My Soul Delighteth in the Scriptures

My Soul *Delighteth* in the Scriptures

Edited by H. Wallace Goddard & Richard H. Cracroft

Bookcraft
Salt Lake City, Utah

Richard Cracroft's "The Pattern of Faith and Jolts of
Joy: Spiritual Surprises" slighty adapted from *A Thoughtful Faith: Essays on Belief by Mormon Scholars,* ed. Philip
L. Barlow (Centerville, Utah: Canon Press, 1986), pp.
293-304.

Bookcraft is a registered trademark of Bookcraft, Inc.

Library of Congress Catalog Card Number 99-72527

ISBN 1-57008-648-6

First Printing, 1999

Printed in the United States of America

CONTENTS

ACKNOWLEDGMENTS

The editors wish to thank Cory H. Maxwell, editorial manager at Bookcraft, Inc., for his wonderfully efficient and professional management of the publication of this book; and Janna DeVore, our editor, of Bookcraft, Inc., for her astute and kindly professional attention to every detail.

FOREWORD

Richard H. Cracroft

The idea for this book arose from a number of impromptu, off-the-cuff, before-and-after meeting gospel chats between (then) Bishop H. Wallace Goddard and me, Richard H. Cracroft, who was at that time serving as Bishop Goddard's High Council advisor in the BYU 62nd Ward, BYU 17th Stake (I'm currently a bishop in the same stake).

Those who know Wally Goddard know him as a profoundly spiritually oriented man. The gospel is always on his mind. He can drop to the heart of a gospel question like few people I know; he then tests possible answers against scriptures which occur to him (because they are always fresh in his mind); then he measures those tentative answers against his extensive personal experience and the observations of other like-minded men and women; he jots down his insights and writes out timely scriptures on an index card that he carries in his shirt pocket; finally, he freely shares his insights with others, humbly, excitedly, infectiously, and in a way, as Huck Finn puts it, "to make a body's mouth water." In fact, talking "gospel" with Wally Goddard is, as you will experience for yourself in his introduction and two essays in this volume, a spiritually mouth-watering experience.

While visiting the meetings of the BYU 62nd Ward, I soon learned that even a perfunctory, after-meeting comment, such as "I liked how the speaker treated [this idea or that principle]," would evoke a probing, "What makes you say that?" from

Bishop Goddard; and before we knew it we would be seated in his office (perhaps at the expense of a Sunday School or priesthood class, I'm afraid) getting at the heart of the matter. These fleeting but refreshing discussions gradually and persuasively proved dead wrong an observation which I made one afternoon early in our relationship. "After all is said and done," I remarked, not-very-sagely, "there aren't very many scriptures which speak to family concerns and problems, are there?"

Bishop Goddard gently questioned the validity of that observation by showing me, through the scriptures, through his own and others' personal experience (even quoting from my own published Church talks!), that which we want to show in this collection of essays in a variety of ways—that, in fact, the holy scriptures abound with patterns, examples, suggestions, applications, insights, instruction, blueprints for personal and family living, and divine solutions for every kind of parental or marital concern or family problem. Indeed, one of the major reasons Nephi could proclaim that "my soul delighteth in the scriptures," is that they have been written, "for the learning and the profit of [our] children"(2 Nephi 4:15). The holy scriptures are, as this book underscores, the spiritual textbooks and divine pattern books for our families.

Filled with faith, hope, and love for our families, each Latter-day Saint stands by the tree of life, "desirous," with Lehi, "that my family should partake of [the fruit] also; for . . . it was desirable above all other fruit"(1 Nephi 8:12). The holy scriptures, deeply felt, carefully pondered, and spiritually discerned, are fraught with divine solutions for individual and family problems and concerns. The essays of this book present many ways in which various Latter-day Saints have discovered the sweet fruit of the gospel in the scriptures and many ways in which they have aided their families to partake and be spiritually refreshed, individually and collectively. Repeatedly and tellingly, these faith-centered writers demonstrate, from various perspectives and rich experience, the importance of making it our daily and holy walk, with Nephi, to "liken all scriptures unto us, that it might be for our profit and learning"(1 Nephi 19:23). The ultimate end of all our endeavors and the purpose of each of these essays is that we, again like Nephi, "might persuade [our families] that they would remember the Lord their Redeemer" (v. 18) all the days of their lives.

INTRODUCTION

H. Wallace Goddard

This book is about how the holy scriptures change lives and bless families. Certainly the scriptures have changed the lives of the Goddard family, although the process, still going on, has zigzagged in a crazy path across the parched deserts and fertile valleys of marriage, children, and foster children. I wish I could say that my instinctive response to every family challenge has been to go to the word for counsel. It has not been. It has been far more common for me to react to any pebble in the road of family life in the same stiff-necked and harsh spirit as Laman and Lemuel. I have wanted life on my terms rather than the Lord's.

Too many times I have sat at challenging scriptural lessons asking with Judas and the Twelve: "Lord, is it I?" (Matthew 26:22). I am wiser to plead, "Shew me thy ways, O Lord; teach me thy paths" (Psalm 25:4). Fortunately the Lord has prolonged the days of my mortal probation so that I can learn (see 2 Nephi 2:21). He never snatches the textbook away from us, even when we are such woeful learners.

Over the years I have seen a pattern emerge in my learning. As I have studied the scriptures, I have been amazed at the hardheartedness of the reluctant followers and non-believers who populate scripture. Can't they see the Lord's way? Next, as I enlarge my appreciation of the powerful lesson that Father is teaching in each scriptural encounter, I wonder that my friends, neighbors, and family members have failed to apply lessons that they so conspicuously need. Finally, after the Lord has prepared my soil through witnessed dramas in scriptures and in my neighbors, He then reaches my reluctant, condescending soul with His vital and personal invitation to greater application of the scripture in my own life. I should not only be polite to strangers but charitable with my frustrated daughter; not only give a generous fast offering but set aside the newspaper to provide time for my son; not only give stirring talks about love but celebrate my wife's unique earnestness with my patient attention; not only appreciate my parents' inspired and wise but imperfect care but forgive them of every flaw and love them. Home is the place where our Christian claims get their severest tests.

The scriptures are designed to help every one of us, individually and in our families. When our children were young, we wanted our scripture study to be suited to their capacities and interests. We selected a quality set of illustrated scripture stories and, every morning before breakfast, told a scripture story with studied passion. The children loved the pictures and seemed to be absorbed by the stories. Because Moses holds a prominent place in scriptural history, we spent weeks studying his life. The time arrived when Moses left his people never to see them again in mortality. One fall morning we told the story of Moses' departure and then proceeded with breakfast. In the middle of breakfast I noticed that four-year-old Andy was crying. I was surprised. "What's wrong, son?" Between sobs he choked out, "Dad, I'm going to miss Moses."

Scriptures can help us create a heavenly culture as we struggle in this telestial world. When family members know Elijah as a humble prophet who was discouraged enough to want to die, it can help them face discouragement. When family members feel Ammon's wonder and awe at declaring "Who could have supposed that our God would have been so merciful as to have snatched us from our awful, sinful, and polluted state?" (Alma 26:17) they are filled with humility and hope. When family members have felt the miracle of Alma's transformation, they know to whom they may look for a mighty change of heart. Those who have felt the heavenly logic of King Benjamin's great address know their responsibility to care for the poor. Those who have studied Jesus' remarkable life know that, in the words of Elder Neal A. Maxwell, "His relentless redemptiveness exceeds our recurring wrongs."[1] The scriptures can change our family culture.

When King Benjamin sent among the vast throng of his people to know if they believed the words of his sermon, "they all cried with one voice, saying: Yea, we believe" (Mosiah 5:2). How can we establish such a culture of belief in our families? It should come as no surprise that the best answers to that question can be found in a familiar scripture.

"And we talk of Christ"

There are many wonderful ways to talk of Christ in our families. Sharing scripture stories is an excellent one. The best way may be prayer. When family members hear one another submit themselves to God, something divine happens. Lewis M. Andrews describes this act of submission: "Lord, I know not what to ask of thee. Thou only knowest what I need. Thou lovest me better than I know how to love myself. Father, give to thy child that which he himself knows not to ask. Smite or heal, depress me or raise me up: I adore all thy purposes without knowing them. I am silent; I offer myself up in a sacrifice; I yield myself to thee; I would have no other desire than to accomplish thy will. Teach me to pray. Pray thyself in me."[2]

"We rejoice in Christ"

We should share our gratitude for the divine with each other. In our home each Sabbath evening we invite family members and visitors to share their best experience of the day. One such Sabbath I tried to capture the miracle I had seen earlier in the day when a discouraged, humble, even desperate, ward member sought counsel from me as her bishop. As I described the miracle I had seen as this woman received hopeful counsel that was wiser than I knew how to give, my voice caught, my eyes filled, and joy ran down my face. My tears were my testimony of an incomprehensibly redemptive Father. Each member of the family, having also felt to sing the song of redeeming love, joined his or her testimony to mine in a similarly liquid fashion.

"We preach of Christ"

We have covenanted that we will "stand as witnesses of God at all times and in all things, and in all places that [we] may be in" (Mosiah 18:9). We may have unexpected opportunities to offer words of hope to colleagues at work. At home we will have many opportunities to "succor the weak, lift up the hands which hang down, and strengthen the feeble knees" (D&C 81:5) if we will let charity overrule correction.

"We prophesy of Christ"

Most of us do not imagine that we are called to prophesy. Indeed, it is not our role as rank and file members of the Church to announce the Second Coming of the Lord. But it is our role, even our obligation, to announce His coming to our own lives. Each week as I sat to write to our missionary children, I was discouraged with the prospect of eking out of my notes of the week anything meaningful. But I determined to make the best of it. As I started to write of the little blessings of the days, I discovered unnoticed miracles and patterns of miracles. By the time I finished writing of the week, I was overwhelmed with awe. "How could He have blessed us so much?" When we open our eyes, we discover that "the mountain [is] full of horses and chariots of fire round about" (2 Kings 6:17) each of us. That is the spirit of prophecy.

"And we write according to our prophecies"

Whether we write in letters, in journals, in essays, or in the "fleshy tables of the heart" (2 Corinthians 3:3), we write so "that our children may know to what source they may look for a remission of their sins" (2 Nephi 25:26).

We do all these things that we and our children may know the Source. The only Source. The Light and Life. The Redeemer. And they can best come to know that Source in the family circle.

Scriptures build a culture of belief; they provide a context for all of our decisions, struggles, sorrows, and joys. They can be a daily blessing. Right now my commonest use of scripture is the index card in my pocket with the words of Alma 36:18: "O Jesus, thou Son of God, have mercy on me." Many times each day I chant Alma's words. I am a better disciple as a result of that frequent and earnest plea for divine help with subduing the natural man. We can tell that the word is taking hold within our hearts when we instinctively interpret all of life through His purposes and we spontaneously trust Him in time of need.

The scriptures can also address specific family problems. My wife is better than I at translating the scriptures into life. For months we had been wrestling with difficult decisions in our family. We had stewed and agonized. One day she called me at work to tell me that she had been seeking answers in the scriptures and had discovered this needed counsel in the Doctrine and Covenants: "Therefore, dearly beloved brethren, let us cheerfully do all things that lie in our power; and then may we stand still, with the utmost assurance, to see the salvation of God, and for his arm to be revealed" (123:17).

What a perfect way to balance faith with responsibility! Only Father could make it so clear. We do all that we can. We do it cheerfully. Then we stand serenely to witness the miracle of His goodness. I am thankful for a companion who uses scripture not only as a context for life's meaning but also for specific and wise counsel. Learning this grand scriptural solution to family problems, we need to teach it to our children, to men and women and children everywhere.

Each family is different in the way it benefits from the scriptures. You will see many of those differences in the diverse chapters of this book. Some families use the scriptures as a road map in all the decisions of life. Some families use the scriptures as fuel to provide hope and purpose. In all instances, finding solutions to family challenges in the scriptures begins with individual insight and inspiration; only then can it be extended and exemplified to those we cherish most. In whatever way we use the scriptures in our lives and in families, this book is intended to help us all learn from the scriptures, to help us learn with more joy and less sorrow as we make the journey back to our eternal home.

NOTES

1. Neal A. Maxwell, "Yearning to Return," *Ensign*, August 1990, p. 24.

2. Lewis M. Andrews, *To Thine Own Self Be True: The Relationship Between Spiritual Values and Emotional Health* (New York: Doubleday, 1987), pp. 62–63.

CHAPTER 1

DIVINE PARENTING:
THE ATONEMENT OF JESUS CHRIST
IS THE KEY

H. Wallace Goddard

HE DOETH NOT ANYTHING SAVE IT BE FOR THE BENEFIT OF
THE WORLD; FOR HE LOVETH THE WORLD, EVEN THAT HE
LAYETH DOWN HIS OWN LIFE THAT HE MAY DRAW ALL MEN UNTO
HIM. WHEREFORE, HE COMMANDETH NONE THAT THEY SHALL
NOT PARTAKE OF HIS SALVATION.

—*2 NEPHI 26:24*

Parenting is what Father does. Caring for His children is the
only thing He does.

"For behold, this is my work and my glory—to bring to pass
the immortality and eternal life of man" (Moses 1:39).

He is the Master Parent, the Perfect Parent! His plan for His
children is aptly called the "great plan of happiness" (Alma
42:8). What can we, as struggling parents, learn from His example
that will help us with our earthly challenges as parents?

Once two dear friends called from a distant city. Their voices
betrayed their exhaustion. "We've had trouble with Breck lately.
We don't know what to do. We're desperate. Will you help us?"
The weary parents described the stresses around their recent move

---

*H. Wallace Goddard is an associate professor of family and human develop-
ment at Utah State University. He has studied teen problem behaviors and
written* The Great Self Mystery *to help teens discover and use their talents.
He and his wife, Nancy, have three children and have had twenty foster children during their married life. He is also the author of* The Frightful and
Joyous Journey of Family Life. *He has twice served as bishop.*

to a new city. The dad's new job entailed long hours, leaving very little time or energy for his family. The mom was overwhelmed with the demands of the move and organizing the household. Six-year-old Breck (his name has been changed) had started acting angry and hostile. Every day he would battle against getting on the bus. He seemed almost to take joy in torturing his mother as she tried to rush him to the school bus that was holding up traffic while he fought his mother. "It seems that he is deliberately trying to manipulate me," observed the frustrated mother. "I think he wants to use his power to control the family. He seems to enjoy it."

Maybe this is the first place in which Satan's mischief is evident in parenting: in the way we assign motives to our children. As adults we credit children with the manipulative and devious motives that we see in ourselves and in most other telestial beings. But the Lord tutors Latter-day Saints with this precious truth about children "Every spirit of man was innocent in the beginning; and God having redeemed man from the fall, men became again, in their infant state, innocent before God" (D&C 93:38).

Because of the redemption, we begin life innocent! Rather than seeing children as little devils to be controlled and managed, Father has taught us that children are little angels to be cherished, protected, and taught. So, how do we explain the deviousness and contrariness that we see in children? Some of it, maybe most of it, is in the eyes of the beholder. "Unto the pure all things are pure: but unto them that are defiled and unbelieving is nothing pure; but even their mind and conscience is defiled" (Titus 1:15). We tend to see in others (especially in our children) what we hate in ourselves.

Still, children do devious, unkind things; they grab toys from other children; they push down children who get in their way. But maybe most of the undesirable behavior we see in children is the child's effort to have his or her needs met. Let's continue looking at the Lord's instruction from Doctrine and Covenants section 93: "And that wicked one cometh and taketh away light and truth, through disobedience, from the children of men, and because of the tradition of their fathers" (v. 39).

We come from Father to earth, "trailing clouds of glory." It does not take long in a telestial world for children to lose some of this light and truth. Part of the trouble comes because *our* parenting behavior is so flawed. But another part of the trouble comes because we cynically underestimate the goodness of our children. When we impute foul motives to our children we then tend to see behaviors that confirm our views. After all, this is a telestial world. We can find troubling behavior in every person on the earth.

"But I have commanded you to bring up your children in light and truth" (D&C 93:40).

Light and truth! When Breck's troubled mother asked me if I believed that he was trying to manipulate her, my instinctive response was, "No. I know Breck. He is an earnest, sweet, normal boy whose worst fault may be that he is tender and a perfectionist. I think he is saying, 'I am so confused about this move! I like to have some order in my life but I have been torn away from friends, our old house, familiar routines . . . and now my mom and dad don't even want to snuggle with me at night because they say I need to be grown up. I feel desperately confused and lonely! Please! Please! Someone help me!'" Identifying Breck as a lonely, confused boy leads to a parenting response very different from the one that would result from identifying him as devious and contrary. Bringing him up in light and truth includes seeing him in the best possible light—as a little boy wanting to be good but feeling very lost, lonely, and overwhelmed at times.

Surprisingly this same principle applies with adolescents who often seem hardened and distant. Stephen R. Covey tells of a father who was estranged from his teen son. The father sought advice from Brother Covey, who recommended sincere and patient listening. The father vowed to try it. But he returned some days later saying that it did not work, the son just would not listen! Brother Covey invited the man to attend a class with him where they would be discussing empathic listening. The man resisted, believing that the son was unreachable, but Brother Covey prevailed. A few days after the class the man returned to Brother Covey again and described an experience with his son. The father had tried to start a discussion with his son but the boy had turned to march angrily from the room. As the boy was leaving the father called out, "Son, you have every reason to be mad. Before you leave, I just want to say how sorry I am for embarrassing you in front of your friends the other day." The boy spun around and exploded, "You will never know how you embarrassed me!" The boy poured out his pain. The father just listened. Patiently. Compassionately. Tearfully. That began a heart-to-heart discussion. When the mother came into the room hours later to invite them to go to bed, the boy responded, "We're not ready to go to bed yet. Dad and I are talking!"[1]

When we get past our judgments and assumptions about our children and when we approach them humbly, we are able to love and bless them. It may take minutes or years to get past our inclinations to judge. But we make it possible by bringing our whole, loving soul as an offering to our children. We can then see tender spirits, who are pained at being so far from Father and in such a miserable world. We can bind up their wounds, offer them peace and love. We can teach them how to feel love, joy, and peace by our examples and our teaching. Here, again, we have the perfect example as described in this scriptural paraphrase: We do not have a high priest who is untouched and unaffected by our infirmities and troubles. We have a high priest who was tempted by every temptation that we can imagine (see Hebrews 4:15). (In fact, He bore every pain and every sorrow of every human who ever lived on the face of the earth!) Since one who has suffered so greatly and so gladly for us is our Heavenly Friend, "Let us therefore come boldly unto the throne of grace, that we may obtain mercy, and find grace to help in time of need" (v. 16).

What a perfect model of the loving, helpful attitude we

should bring to our children! Jesus taught of a good Samaritan who healed the injured traveler by pouring wine and oil into his wounds and by carrying him to a home where he could be cared for. Clearly the good Samaritan represents Jesus, who binds up all our wounds without thought of our ability to repay Him and without thought of our deservedness. And He carries us to the inn with the promise to provide whatever is necessary for a complete healing. We may offer the same healing compassion to our children.

Knowing that we should offer redeeming love to our children, how do parents control their behavior? Over the course of my friends' first month in their new home, Breck had become increasingly anxious. He did not sleep well. He cried more. He threw tantrums, banged walls, and clung to his parents. He became sassy, defiant, and physical. The night before our phone conversation, dinnertime had become a battleground. Breck spit out some food. He was told that he would not be able to have a cookie if he misbehaved. He pushed his chair over, began screaming, raged around the room, and punched his parents when they tried to calm him. He was told to get control of himself or there would be no family night. He bit his Dad. Mom and Dad carried him to his bed and held him down for more than an hour while the frenzied boy threatened to get his knife and cut their necks. Desperate and tearful, the dad gave a priesthood blessing to his son while he held him down.

These sweet and beautiful parents grieved over their son's ugly outburst. What can parents do in such challenges? To get some ideas, let's jump forward to that time when Jesus will present us to the Father. He has painted a very vivid picture of that drama in Doctrine and Covenants section 45. "Listen to him who is the advocate [*Advocate!* Not accuser, but advocate!] with the Father, who is pleading your cause [Pleading my cause? Thanks be to heaven!] before him" (v. 3).

We might half expect that Jesus will take us to the Father and apologetically present us. "You know, Father, here is Wally. He was a pretty good guy. He tried hard. Yeah, I know. He made a lot of mistakes. In fact, he made some really stupid mistakes! But he tried hard and he did a few good things." In our telestial way of thinking, we almost imagine that Jesus will weakly plead our cause and then step out of the way to see if we can cut some kind of deal with a Father who has every reason to be disappointed with us. But that is not what He does! Jesus describes His pleading for us: "Father, behold the sufferings and death of him who did no sin, in whom thou wast well pleased; behold the blood of thy Son which was shed, the blood of him whom thou gavest that thyself might be glorified" (D&C 45:4).

Being mortals we rather expect Him to follow this grand presentation of Himself by suggesting that He be given the best seat in the heavenly house and that maybe some of His best buddies be admitted under His merit. Once again He surprises us. After presenting the inexpressible merits of His goodness, He steps behind us and pushes us to Father: "Wherefore, Father, spare these my brethren that believe on my name, that they may come unto me and have everlasting life" (D&C 45:5).

Hold everything! After presenting the merits of His remarkable goodness, He applies that goodness to us so that we can join Him and Father in the heavenly home? He lived, taught, suffered, and died only so that He could rescue us? "*Who could have supposed* that our God would have been so merciful as to have snatched us from our awful, sinful, and polluted state?" (Alma 26:17; emphasis added).

This is all well and good—but how do we apply this to such gritty problems as Breck's outburst? Notice in the parents' behavior the human tendency to threaten: "If you continue to spit out your food you will not be given a cookie. If you continue to act up we will not have home evening." That is all very natural. And, unfortunately, "the natural man is an enemy to God" (Mosiah 3:19). Our automatic reactions in a telestial world are almost always wrong.

Rather than accuse, confront, and threaten, parents might respond to the message of pain and confusion that the boy's behavior represent. They can help the troubled boy against their common enemies of confusion, alienation, and fear. His father might say, "Wow! Son, you are really angry. Shall we run around the block together so that you can show me your anger?" Or Mother might say, "Son, this all seems so confusing. Can we snuggle together in the rocking chair?" There are probably many more ideas that are still better. Parents are uniquely qualified, based on experience and inspiration, to know what will work with that child under this or that circumstance. There are many responses that might help the boy deal with his immediate anger and confusion.

Long-term solutions to help the boy might include arranging for the mother to volunteer at school so that she could be with her boy during the difficult weeks of transition at a new school. Dad might carve out some time for his son on the weekends. Mom might have the boy stay home from school with her once a week to have time together for a picnic. To help him build new friendships, the parents might invite one of their son's classmates over to play at the house after school. They might invite their son to make a schedule of special times he would like to have and to tell family members how they can help him make his new life in his new neighborhood feel safe and satisfying. The role of an advocate is to use our resources—our calmness, creativity, affection, and hope—to help rather than to use our human peevishness, to judge, confront, and condemn.

Unquestionably, there are times when we must set limits on children's behavior. But if we do that without love, it will not be effective. "For the letter killeth, but the spirit giveth life" (2 Corinthians 3:6). If I could go back and do one thing differently with our children, it would be to invest far more in loving and far less in lecturing. It makes me tired when I think about the lectures and consequences that I heaped on my earnest little children.

Intriguingly, Breck's mother told a story about him that spoke volumes about his intentions. At Breck's school each student started the day with five tokens. Any child who misbehaved lost a token. Every day Breck returned home and reported that he had not lost any tokens. He seemed to be very anxious about the prospect that he might lose one someday. Breck's statements fit a picture of a boy who is trying very hard but who feels overwhelmed and anxious. Each child acts up for different reasons—maybe out of anger, out of not knowing better, or out of loneliness. Breck was clearly acting up because he was desperately confused.

When children cannot find a good way to have their needs met, they may resort to terrorism—not out of meanness but out of desperation. Perhaps, rather than wanting power over the family, Breck really wanted to feel a little power in his own life. Maybe he wasn't trying to manipulate and punish the family, but asserting that he wants to feel loved and safe.

When Breck threatened, while thrashing against parental restraint, to cut his parents' necks, they painfully responded that that would kill them. He promptly amended his threat to cutting their arms. Breck really did not want to destroy his parents. Rather, he desperately wanted help to feel safe and loved.

We can learn much about healing troubled family members by Jesus' example. A father brought his son to Jesus for healing. Since the time of the boy's birth an evil spirit had thrown the boy into fires and waters and had almost destroyed him. The boy and his family had agonized for years. The father had done all he knew to help his tortured son. The tender father's frantic plea to Jesus touches the heart of any person who has ever been anxious for the well-being of a loved one: "If thou canst do any thing, have compassion on us, and help us" (Mark 9:22).

How did Jesus respond to the plea? He taught the man the condition for all healing. "If thou canst believe, all things are possible to him that believeth" (Mark 9:23). Healing comes through believing on the Great Physician.

What was the humble father's response? Did he chafe, "Well, I believe as much as the next guy"? Did he take offense and complain, "To tell you the truth, I don't think that believing in you is going to make one whit of difference in my son's well-being"? No.

"And straightway the father of the child cried out, and said with tears, Lord, I believe; help thou mine unbelief" (Mark 9:24).

That sweet father seemed to say, "Lord, I want to believe. I try to believe. Please, give me the gift of believing." And Jesus, having made the requirement of belief, stands ready to give us even that gift of believing! Never was one more gracious than He!

With the father's cry for help, Jesus rebuked the foul spirit. The boy appeared to be dead. But, just as with us, Jesus reached down, "took him by the hand, and lifted him up" (Mark 9:27).

This has everything to do with parenting! If we want to be healed of the injuries we have suffered in our lives, we may call on Him for healing. If we want to be healed of our unkind and ungenerous feelings for our children, we may call on Him to be healed. He will lift us up to see as He sees, love as He loves, and bless as He blesses. In this hellish world no parent can ever parent as he or she should without that divine help.

We had talked about Breck for almost two hours when an exhausted father sighed, "Wally, do you think I've ruined my son? Has my perfectionism doomed him to a lifetime of anxiety and frustration?"

My soul exploded: "No! No. You are the ideal father for Breck. You have wrestled for a lifetime with your own perfectionism. You have recently made great breakthroughs in your struggle. You continue to discover and rediscover the inexpressible goodness of God to help you. Is there anyone better on the face of the earth to help Breck than one who has wrestled with the same challenges for a lifetime? Besides, you are almost thirty as you confront this imperfection. You can help Breck begin much sooner. With the testimony that you have of Jesus' remarkable redemption, you can offer your son divine hope along with practical helps. The painful challenges you have in your relationship with Breck underscore your need for Jesus' eternal perspective on your son and your unique preparation to help Breck."

We seem perfectly suited to make each other crazy in families. Sometimes that irony seems too painful. But, if we have faith, we suspect that there is "divine design and purpose" in our family experiences and relationships. We are put together in families because we are uniquely able to bless each other. Maybe adult faith can be defined as the stubborn resolve to see God's goodness in every part of our lives. "Let the kaleidoscope of life's circumstances be shaken again and again," wrote Elder Neal A. Maxwell, "and the 'true believer in Christ' will still see 'with the eye of faith' divine design and purpose in his life."[2] Everything in our lives can bless us. Maybe each of us has the life curriculum that is perfect for us. After all, Father is determined to make something wonderful out of us. At times that may be very inconvenient, even painful. But, seen from an eternal perspective, it will make joyous sense.

How do we know if we are doing well enough as parents? I have often said to myself, "some parents seem to do so well, while I fumble along, making so many mistakes! What is wrong with me?" I take comfort in the Lord's startling definition of righteousness found in Luke:

> And he spake this parable unto certain which trusted in themselves that they were righteous [parents], and despised others:
>
> Two men went up into the temple to pray; the one a Pharisee, and the other a publican.
>
> The Pharisee stood and prayed thus with himself, God, I thank thee, that I am not as other men are, extortioners, unjust, adulterers, or even as this publican. [And I am thankful that my children are not on drugs or in trouble with the law.]
>
> I fast twice in the week, I give tithes of all that I possess. [We hold regular family home evening, and family prayer.]
>
> And the publican, standing afar off, would not lift up so much as his eyes unto heaven, but smote upon his breast, saying, God be merciful to me a sinner. [I make so many mistakes! I lose my temper, I fail to understand my children, I neglect prayer.]
>
> I tell you, this [parent] went down to his house justified rather than the other: for every one that exalteth himself shall be abased;

and he that humbleth himself shall be [Note this key word for Latter-
day Saints:] *exalted*. (18:9–14; emphasis added)

It is not the parent who seems to do it all perfectly who will
be exalted. It is the one who recognizes his own failings and calls
upon Father with all the energy of his heart. Parenting classes
may give us good ideas for dealing with children. Talking with
wise and tender friends may help us, but, if we are to excel at
parenting we must have divine help.

Shortly before he died, Lehi summarized his life experience:
"But behold, the Lord hath redeemed my soul from hell; I have
beheld his glory, and I am encircled about eternally in the arms
of his love" (2 Nephi 1:15).

Many of us will conclude our parenting experience saying
something very similar: "The Lord has redeemed my soul from
the hell of a telestial world and my persistent imperfections. As
He has refined me and blessed those I have tried to serve, I have
witnessed His glory. Now, as I finish my mortal struggle, I am
encircled about eternally in the arms of His perfect love."

It should come as no surprise that some of the greatest trials of our lives come in parenting and family life. Only a task
that demands the sacrifice of all our pride, all our self-importance,
all our stubbornness has the power to make us perfect. Our
family challenges on earth prepare us for fulness of family joy
where we will enjoy not only our earthly family but also the
throngs of loved ones whom we have not seen since our earth
lives began. At that great day every knee will bow and every
tongue will confess, not because His power commands it but
because we are astonished and humbled by His inexpressible
goodness and wisdom.

It is a good beginning to know His remarkable goodness,
but it is not enough. Joseph Smith reported the following vision.
"I saw the Twelve Apostles of the Lamb, who are now upon the
earth, who hold the keys of this last ministry, in foreign lands,
standing together in a circle, much fatigued, with their clothes
tattered and feet swollen, with their eyes cast downward, and

Jesus standing in their midst, and they did not behold Him. The Savior looked upon them and wept."[3]

Very often in our parenting experiences we may be weary and downcast. We may not realize that the Savior is in our midst, ready to help us; we may not understand how we can draw His power into our family life. But there is much we can do.

1. *We can draw on His power by being humble.* Alma the Younger provides the great example of being transformed by humility. He was desperately miserable when he reflected on his many sins. He says that he was filled with "inexpressible horror" (Alma 36:14), hoping to "be banished and become extinct" (v. 15), and was "racked, even with the pains of a damned soul" (v. 16), even "racked with torment" (v. 17); he called on Jesus as his only hope when he recollected his father's teachings. "I remembered also to have heard my father prophesy unto the people concerning the coming of one Jesus Christ, a Son of God, to atone for the sins of the world. Now, as my mind caught hold upon this thought, I cried within my heart: O Jesus, thou Son of God, have mercy on me, who am in the gall of bitterness, and am encircled about by the everlasting chains of death" (vv. 17–18).

Our desperation in parenting is very useful if it leads us to call upon Jesus in total humility. We may remember the greatness of God, and our own nothingness, and humble ourselves, calling on the name of the Lord daily (see Mosiah 4:11). We may call out, "Father, I'm trying so hard and doing so imperfectly! Please, help me! Please pour out thy perfect grace on my weak soul!" There is a surprising peace that settles in on us when we stop trying to be super-parents and recognize our dependence upon God.

2. *We can draw on His power by having faith in His ability to bless us and our children in every experience.* The Lord modestly reminds us that He is able to do His own work (see 2 Nephi 27:20). Even the child who drives us crazy is a gift from God to refine us.

Just as Nephi, we are turned from despair to peace when we "know in whom [we] have trusted" (2 Nephi 4:19). There is a serenity, even an optimism, that settles in on us as we accept the truth that He will never lose track of us. "Can a woman forget her sucking child, that she should not have compassion on the son of her womb? yea, they may forget, yet will I not forget thee" (Isaiah 49:15).

Adult faith, the kind necessary for effective parenting goes beyond acknowledging that He exists. It celebrates His remarkable ability to turn everything to our good and to provide us with every lesson necessary for exaltation. We call upon Father and trust serenely, knowing that He will provide the experiences that will bless and perfect us.

Elder Neal A. Maxwell radiates that faith in Father's perfect ability to tutor us when he writes: "One's life, therefore, is brevity compared to eternity—like being dropped off by a parent for a day at school. But what a day!"[4]

3. *We can draw on His power when we gladly repent.* No parent gets it right the first time. We all make lots of mistakes. Consider this wise counsel from Moroni: "Yea, teach parents that they must repent and be baptized, and humble themselves as their little children, and they shall all be saved with their little children" (Moroni 8:10).

Amaleki counsels us to "come unto [Christ], and offer your whole souls as an offering unto him, and continue in fasting and praying, and endure to the end; and as the Lord liveth ye will be saved" (Omni 1:26).

Repentance is more than making the same mistake over and over again and feeling bad about it. Father expects us to keep looking for better ways. We observe and seek counsel from those who seem to exemplify the teachings of Jesus. We yearn to find better ways. We study Jesus' life for the perfect example. Repenting is learning.

4. *We can draw on His power when we endure.* Sometimes family processes require great patience and endurance. I once listened to a man who had been married for decades and was telling me that he loved his wife dearly, but was not sure if she loved him. Yet he was fully content to take joy in loving. I think we are always wise to keep offering our best even when it is not

returned. Sometimes it takes a very long time for us to find again the bread that we cast upon the water. We may follow the perfect example of Father: "And how merciful is our God unto us, . . . and he stretches forth his hands unto them all the day long" (Jacob 6:4). Patience is a vital dimension of godliness.

5. *We can draw on His power when we love with the perfect love that we call charity.* An ancient commandment was given to love our neighbors as ourselves. But Jesus gave a higher law to His dearest disciples. After washing the feet of His Apostles, and only hours before giving His life for them, He invited: "A new commandment I give unto you, That ye love one another; *as I have loved you*, that ye also love one another. By this shall all men know that ye are my disciples, if ye have love one to another" (John 13:34–35; emphasis added).

How is it possible to love as He loves? How is it possible to be like Him who loved and sacrificed His life for us? Moroni provides the answer: "Pray unto the Father with all the energy of heart, that ye may be filled with this love, which he hath bestowed upon all who are true followers of his Son" (Moroni 7:48). For us to have this pure love, this charity that Christ has, requires a divine gift. When we are filled up with Jesus, then, and only then, can we love as He loves. He loves through us. It is a sweet miracle. Every parent should pray earnestly to see his or her children as Jesus sees them, to love them as He loves them. Family life stretches us beyond our capacity so that we will draw on His divine power. That is the challenge for which family life is perfectly designed.

So, the Atonement of Jesus Christ has everything to do with our effectiveness as parents. It allows us to be born into this world innocent. It provides the power for us to come to Christ in faith and to be filled with that perfect love that we call charity. It provides the power for us to be changed, cleansed, refreshed, renewed, and filled with divine nature. It provides the power to rescue us from our sins of attitude and action. And Jesus' life of love and service provides the perfect example for us to study. Jesus and His Atonement provide the only hope for us as parents, the only way for us to be at one with Him and with beloved family members.

NOTES

1. See Stephen R. Covey, *The 7 Habits of Highly Effective Families* (New York: Golden Books, 1997), pp. 13–14.

2. Neal A. Maxwell, "'True Believers in Christ'," *1980 Devotional Speeches of the Year* (Provo: Brigham Young University, 1981), p. 139.

3. Joseph Smith, Jr., in *History of the Church,* 2:381.

4. Neal A. Maxwell, "Premortality, a Glorious Reality," *Ensign,* November 1985, p. 15.

CHAPTER 2

CHICKENHEART

Lael Littke

We come to the scriptures in different ways and at different ages. I came as a child when I needed an answer to a heavy problem. My mother wisely opened the scriptures to give me that answer, thus starting me on a lifelong quest to seek wisdom from those holy books.

I was amazed at that time by what could be found in the scriptures. Being a child, I found most of it beyond my understanding. But I loved the beauty of the words my mother read to me and my siblings, and I memorized many of my favorite passages. As I grew older I found those remembered verses coming to my aid as I tried to deal with life. The word of God became my center, the final authority when a question arose. And I am still amazed at what can be found therein.

When I married and gave birth to a daughter, I read to her from the scriptures, following the example of my mother. I know they have suggested solutions for her just as they have done for me ever since the year my life changed and I realized I was a chickenheart.

Lael Littke is a full-time writer who lives in Pasadena, California, with six cats and two dogs. She has one married daughter who also lives in California. She is the author of more than thirty books for teenagers and younger readers, and has published books in the LDS and national markets. Her most recent books include the Bee There *series for LDS readers and* What About Lenore?

Up until I was seven my life had been pleasant and pre-
dictable, with a constant, seasonal pattern. In the winter we went
to school. Under the summer moon we played night games in
the orchard and fields. All year-round we attended church each
week in the lovely redbrick chapel on Schoolhouse Hill there in
Mink Creek, Idaho. Sometimes we went to movies in Preston.
This was our life.

Besides our own family we had a bonus family, because Dad
and Uncle Dan, who lived just across the road, were brothers;
and Mama and Aunt Mahalia were sisters. There were four children in our family, seven in theirs, and our two families were as
one. To us kids both houses were home. We ate and slept at
whichever house we happened to be when the time came.

My cousin Wayne was the oldest child of the two families,
and when I was seven the big change came about when he went
away to college.

I wasn't in favor of it. We couldn't spare him. He was the
one who held my hand in the scary darkness the first time I was
allowed to play "Run Sheep Run" with the older kids. He was
the one who gave me an identity by showing me that Mink
Creek was on the map of Idaho. ("This little dot," he said.
"That's where we live." And my heart swelled with pride because
if anybody ever said "There isn't any such place as Mink Creek,"
I could point to the map and show him a thing or two. It said
right there in tiny black letters: *Mink Creek*.)

Nobody in Dad and Uncle Dan's families had ever gone to
college. The five brothers had settled all in a row in a narrow little
valley with Strawberry Creek flowing down the center. They
farmed the sidehills and the tops of the hills and around the foot
of the hills. It was a hard life. All of us kids worked from the time
we were old enough to ride the derrick horse. But it was a good
life and we loved one another. How *could* Wayne want to leave?

"Why do you have to go?" I wailed to him.

"I like to learn," he said. "There is so much in the world to
know."

But he already knew so much. He was always studying when

he wasn't doing chores. He was the valedictorian of his class in our little school.

Aunt Mahalia and Mama were proud. "He's the first to go out into the outside world," Aunt Mahalia said. "I wish we could give him more than hope and homemade bread to take along." "He'll be all right," Mama said. "He's a great example to the other kids." Nodding, Aunt Mahalia said, "He's our bellwether." ("What's a bellwether?" I asked. "A bellwether is the sheep that leads the rest of the flock," Mama said. "He wears a bell so that the others will know where he is." And I wondered for days if Wayne would wear a bell when he went off to college in the outside world so that we would know where he was.)

I was frightened by his leaving. If he was the bellwether, did that mean the other kids would follow him? What about Joan? She would graduate from high school soon. And my sister Ivonne. No, not Ivonne. She couldn't leave. I would be afraid to sleep alone in our room away upstairs. (I thought about Mama's "away upstairs" song. It told of a little boy who wouldn't say his prayers, and when he went to bed at night away upstairs, his papa heard him holler and his mama heard him bawl, and when they turned the covers down, *he wasn't there at all!* If Ivonne left, I *couldn't* forget to say my prayers anymore the way I some- times did.)

Would *all* of us kids go off into the *outside world* the way Wayne was going to do? What about me? Oh never, not ever me. I was afraid. I was chicken. Chickenhearted.

The years went by. Joan and Ivonne left home to work in Preston, but they came home on weekends so the pattern of our lives was not changed too much. Wayne graduated from college. I was eleven then, and as proud as the rest of the family of our bellwether (who didn't after all have to wear a bell), with all that knowledge in his head. He'd been born in a two-room house in an obscure dot of a town, but now he was a college graduate. Why, Abraham Lincoln had been a farm boy, born in a cabin, and he had become president of the United States! He hadn't even gone to college the way Wayne had. Maybe someday I could point to a picture of the president of the United States and say, "He's my cousin. The president. He's my cousin Wayne."

There was nothing that could hold Wayne back now.

But there was. He planned to stay home for a year to earn money to go on to even more school. On a cold December day he went up into the hills to get a load of wood for a neighbor and was killed by a falling log.

My brother Varon and I knew something was wrong when we got home from school to find our house cold and dark, with no pleasant cooking smells filling the kitchen, no fire in the old coal range. No Mama and little brother Georgie to greet us. No Dad to wave to us from the barn.

They came soon, crying and broken, and my little chicken-heart shrank away from the words they were saying. Wayne killed. Dead. Gone to where he could never come back home for Christmas or a weekend dance. The world was an ugly, fearsome place, and somehow I had to convince the rest of our family never to leave the safety of our mountains.

But even that was no guarantee. The accident had happened right there on the slopes of our mountains. Right there in Mink Creek. So was there no safety anywhere?

The long black hearse picked up Wayne from the hillside and came back to our houses before heading for Preston. "Would you like to see him?" the driver asked gently.

Her hand over her mouth, Aunt Mahalia nodded.

I hid my head. I didn't want to look at Death. My chicken-heart would stop if I did.

But I did look, expecting to see something hideous and frightening.

But it wasn't Death lying there on the stretcher. It was Wayne. Wayne, still wearing the blue overalls and denim jacket I'd seen that morning as I climbed aboard the schoolbus. Wayne, his wavy, red-gold hair ruffling a little in the slight breeze. My cousin Wayne, with all that knowledge that would never now be used for anything.

There was a funeral. (Even now, a lifetime later, I can't smell lilies or hear the hymn "I Need Thee Every Hour" without feeling again the emotions of that terrible first loss.)

Several days after the funeral I came upon Uncle Dan sitting on his front steps. His head was bowed and his rough farmer's hands dangled between his knees.

I sat down beside him. "It's not fair," I said. "Wayne worked so hard for all that knowledge. It's not fair that it's all gone to waste."

Uncle Dan looked up in surprise. "Gone to waste?" he said. "It's not gone to waste."

"Yes, it is," I said bitterly. "He's dead."

Uncle Dan nodded. "Yes," he said. "He's gone on to another life. But all that knowledge and learning went with him. They'll be his for eternity. Those things and the love of his family."

What? What was this he was telling me?

"Are you sure?" I asked.

"Ask your mother," he said.

I did. Mama was the authority on the four black books on the top shelf of the bookcase. Holy Bible was the title of the thickest book. Book of Mormon was another. There were two other slimmer volumes: Doctrine and Covenants, and The Pearl of Great Price. I had peeked into the books, since anything with words was of interest to me. But the pages were fragile and the writing small. I didn't try to understand it.

I told Mama what Uncle Dan had said. She took down the Doctrine and Covenants and flipped through the pages. "Here." Stabbing a finger at a page she read, "Section 130, verses 18 and 19. 'Whatever principle of intelligence we attain unto in this life, it will rise with us in the resurrection. And if a person gains more knowledge and intelligence in this life through his diligence and obedience than another, he will have so much the advantage in the world to come."

Mama wiped her eyes on the hem of her apron as she read.

I strained to understand the words. I had heard of resurrection. In fact, my older brother Varon had told me about it and we'd done an experiment, burying a dead robin in a cocoa can with a tight fitting lid. A year later we'd dug it up and looked inside to see if the robin had resurrected. It was still there, decayed and smelly. Varon said it was because we'd put the lid on too tight and it couldn't get out, which scared me so bad I vowed I would never die and be put into a coffin.

Wayne was dead and buried, but Mama told me his spirit was not in the ground in the cemetery behind our redbrick church. It had gone on to another place, she said.

And now I knew that he had taken with him everything he had learned in our little school as well as in college. And he'd learned so much that certainly he would have a whole lot of advantage. Maybe he was even a teacher in that "world to come" where he was now. I couldn't think of anything more exalted than being a teacher. My cousin Wayne, a teacher. That was even better than being president.

My chickenheart quailed a little as I thought ahead. "Maybe we should all go off to the outside world," I said. "Maybe we should all go to college."

"I hope you can," Mama said.

Time passed. I learned that the scriptures contained a lot more than just the simple Bible stories I'd heard in Sunday School and Primary. I learned that even those stories were not as simple as they seemed. "What do we learn from the story of Noah?" my Sunday School teacher asked. "To be obedient when the Lord tells us to do something," we said, and my chickenheart quivered in fright as I wondered what I would do if the Lord asked me to do something.

"How will I know what the Lord wants me to do?" I asked Mama.

"Look in the Bible," Mama said. "First Kings, chapter 19, verses 11 and 12."

By now I could puzzle out the meaning of much of the scriptures. I looked where she told me and read: "And, behold, the Lord passed by, and a great and strong wind rent the mountains, and brake in pieces the rocks before the Lord; but the Lord was not in the wind: and after the wind an earthquake; but the Lord was not in the earthquake: And after the earthquake a fire; but the Lord was not in the fire: and after the fire a still small voice."

I read the passage again, and yet again, savoring the sound of the words. The wind—I knew the wind. Sometimes it roared down out of the canyon north of us and blew down the big trees on our lawns. I knew earthquakes. Although we didn't get many in Idaho, we'd had more than a couple of real dish rattlers. And fire. Terrifying, out of control fire that burned down barns and haystacks and sometimes even houses. I knew fire.

But the Lord was not in the wind, or earthquake, or fire. What I needed to listen for was the still small voice. Gentle and quiet. Not to be dreaded, not to be afraid of. Just listened to.

I filed that away with the quote from the Doctrine and Covenants about the resurrection. My chickenheart rested easier.

But a new trial came upon us. It arrived in Mink Creek just as it did in hundreds of other small towns as well as large cities on a December Sunday, exploding through the radio speakers and assaulting our unbelieving ears.

"Pearl Harbor," the radio screamed. "Bombs are falling. Ships are sinking."

We stood around the radio, white-faced, trying to understand. Dad was away, hauling the farmers' milk to Preston as he did every day of the week. I felt unprotected, my chickenheart fluttering.

"What does it mean, Mama?" I whispered.

"It means war," Mama said.

I peered anxiously through the window at the snow-covered hills outside. War. The word conjured up a vision of some monstrous, clanking machine, and I half expected to see it grinding its way across the ridges and through the ravines of our mountains.

"The boys will all have to go," Ivonne said. She and Joan were home for the weekend from their jobs in Preston. Our families were complete, with everybody home except for Wayne, dead now for a year. "The boys we date. The boys we dance with."

Varon was just sixteen. He wouldn't have to go. Surely the war would be over before he had to go.

Quickly 1941 slid off the calendar, and we were into 1942. By now places like Mindanao and Luzon and Corregidor were household words.

My chickenheart pulsed with fright. So far the war hadn't affected our two families much. But the boys, those boys Ivonne and Joan and Anna Beth had danced with, they were off in far-flung places being shot at. Some county boys had already been killed, as reported in the Preston newspaper. And Varon's eighteenth birthday, draft age, was coming closer.

"I'm afraid," I told Mama. "Bad things are happening."

She didn't deny it.

"What can we do?" I wailed.

"Have faith," Mama said. "Pray. Trust in the Lord."

I pulled the thickest of the black books off the shelf and started reading.

"Cast thy burden upon the Lord," I read in Psalm 55:22, "and he shall sustain thee."

I liked Psalms. I read more. I liked Psalm 37:7, which said, "Rest in the Lord, and wait patiently for him." In Psalm 128:1–2, I read, "Blessed is every one that feareth the Lord; that walketh in his ways. For thou shalt eat the labour of thine hands: happy shalt thou be, and it shall be well with thee." And the greatest comfort of them all, the graceful, flowing twenty-third Psalm: "The Lord is my shepherd; I shall not want."

I was uplifted. Sustained. I trusted and prayed.

Joan and Ivonne joined the WAVES and went away to do their part in the war effort. Anna Beth joined the WAACS.

And Varon went to war after all, drafted in February of 1944 when he completed requirements for high school graduation. After basic training, he was sent to the European theater of operations, and I was more afraid than I'd ever been before. If

Wayne had been killed right there in our own little town, what hideous things could happen to Varon on the other side of the world?

He was seriously wounded in France just before his nine-teenth birthday, shot through the elbow and side, the bullet barely missing a kidney.

He came home several months later, with a stiffened arm and old eyes.

But *he came home*. Home to our mountains. "I will lift up mine eyes," I read in Psalm 121:1–2, "unto the hills, from whence cometh my help. My help cometh from the Lord, which made heaven and earth." And in verse 7 I read, "The Lord shall preserve thee from all evil: he shall preserve thy soul."

I knew now that bad things could happen anywhere. Bad things *had* happened. But we had survived as a family. I no longer expected miracles from the world. ("Maybe," Aunt Mahalia said, "the biggest miracle is that more good things happen than bad.") But I had our families and the comfort of the scriptures to firm up my chickenheart.

Eventually I left that chickenheart behind me, along with the stick horses of my childhood and my collection of marbles and my doll, Carol (because I'd gotten her for Christmas one year). It was my turn to go off into the *outside world*. I was no longer afraid. In fact, I looked forward to the adventures that were to come. I would be all right. (I knew to listen for the still small voice, didn't I?)

Wayne, even though dead, was indeed my bellwether. I sought knowledge, a college degree, a career in writing. Then I found a worthy husband, gave birth to a beloved daughter, lived in many of the large cities of the United States. I continued learning, about parenting, homemaking, people, writing, the world, life. This is what I will take with me when I journey to that "other world" where now most of my family, including my husband, await me. Someday I will go on to meet them. I am not afraid.

"For I know that my redeemer liveth, and that he shall stand at the latter day upon the earth; And though after my skin worms destroy this body, yet in my flesh shall I see God" (Job 19:25–26).

CHAPTER 3

TRACING FATHER'S PATTERNS: TAKING "ONE STEP INTO THE DARK"

Richard H. Cracroft

We are surrounded by patterns. Our children learn to live, just as we do, and as our parents did before us, by discovering, identifying, tracing, and following patterns. We awaken in the morning to the sun's diurnal pattern; our bodies function and malfunction in patterns predicated by our patterned DNA. Our formal and informal schooling consists of learning, testing, and repeating proven patterns. Our sciences and mathematics are centered in formulaic patterns, and so are our works of art, drama, music, dance, and literature. Our games, from hopscotch and Monopoly to chess and football, are simply patterned play. And coming to know our Heavenly Father, "the only true God, and Jesus Christ, whom [He] has sent" (John 17:3), is really coming to discern, learn, test, and apply celestial patterns over the patterns of a telestial world. Because we are pattern-centered and pattern-driven beings, teaching our families to discern and trace our Heavenly Father's patterns among the other patterns in

Richard H. Cracroft is a professor of English at BYU and director of the Center for the Study of Christian Values in Literature. Currently a bishop, he has served as a stake president and president of the Switzerland Zürich Mission. Richard and his wife, Janice, live in Provo. They are the parents of three children: Richard, Jeffrey, and Jennifer.

our lives is an exciting, blessed and lifelong endeavor for every mortal mother and father. The reward for teaching and modeling divine pattern-tracing is that our confidence and that of our family members will "wax strong in the presence of God" (D&C 121:45), forever.

A *pattern* is a model, form, format, template, example, overlay, or paradigm of an object, process, behavior, act, or character trait that we deem deserving of imitation and that is arranged so as to enable you or me or him or her to follow, reproduce, imitate, replicate, trace, copy, or repeat the qualities or the spiritual characteristics of the original or prototype in a way that remains unchanged and unchanging. Divine patterns are, then, the processes, fundamental laws, principles, and truths that the Lord seems to follow in ordering and organizing His heavenly and earthly realms—at least as far as we can detect them from our finite and very limited perspectives.

Our Heavenly Father's plan for His mortal children, His gospel, is essentially His divine pattern, a pattern which, if followed, will lead us to our eternal home. In a variety of ways, our Father reveals His patterns of truth and righteousness to His individual mortal children, according to His will and purposes and according to their desire, ability, and readiness to understand. The Holy Spirit, who is Father's messenger to His mortal children, enables us to discern, identify, and understand those patterns necessary for our personal growth. The Holy Spirit urges us to follow, trace, copy, or imitate the patterns which will cleanse our souls of earth stain, crack through accumulated earth crust, and purify our souls as we retrace the Father's patterns back to our heavenly home.

In June, 1831, the Lord showed the Prophet Joseph Smith the importance He attaches to divine patterns. After disclosing some of His patterns relating to missionary work, the Lord told the young Prophet, "I will give unto you a pattern in all things, that ye may not be deceived" (D&C 52:14). He suggests that there are patterns "in all things," and He implies that tracing such patterns is important. As part of His grand design, you and

I and our family members are presently taking our turns on earth. We come to these parentheses in eternity shorn of everything but our customized spiritual DNA, which has been designed by Father to assist us in transforming the human compromise we have become into the men and women of God we formerly were and will yet be (only more so). That spirit within us is intuitively analogical—that is, our spirits enjoy built-in pattern detectors, which enable us to see similarities or analogies between things around us here on earth and things of the eternal, spiritual world. Our divine spirits, then, help us to trace the divine "pattern in all things."

Tracking the spiritual patterns of our Heavenly Father is, in fact, one of the important spiritual exercises we can practice and teach our families to practice. Indeed, "All things unto me are spiritual" (D&C 29:34), the Lord told the Prophet Joseph. And that same Lord, speaking to Moses as Jehovah, explained not only that "all things . . . are spiritual," but revealed that "all things have their likeness, and all things are created and made to bear record of me. . . : all things bear record of me" (Moses 6:63). Here, then, is a key pattern which we ought to teach our children in every teaching moment, in every family home evening, until it becomes an automatic spiritual response: we should be ready to discern, in all times and places, those hints and intimations and those direct and indirect evidences of the patterns of our God. For the spiritually discerning man and woman, this world becomes a kind of Urim and Thummim that enables those who allow themselves to be schooled by the Holy Spirit to look at the earth and its inhabitants through spiritual spectacles and see beyond the part to the whole. Gradually, then, the spiritually-minded child of God begins to discern divine patterns everywhere, for, as the popular ballad asserts, "On a clear day you can see forever."

The holy scriptures, which are God's great pattern books–His divine *Butterick*, *Vogue*, or *McCalls'* compendium of patterns—enable us who are willing to awaken in response to the Spirit's nudgings, to trace, test, and cut those patterns in the fabric of our own mortal experiences. It is imperative, then, for us who are mothers and fathers not only to master those pattern books but to introduce and teach them to our children and their families, to assist them in quickening and establishing in their souls the spiritual discernment and understanding requisite to tracing the divine hand and eternal patterns of our Father as they appear in this transient and mutable mortal world. Finding and pondering and acting on the abundant evidences of divine patterns reveals to us not only some wonderful hints about the divine order and nature of existence, but provides mortal pattern seekers with another way in which we can experience firsthand the presence and power of the Godhead.

Because the holy scriptures are the foundation of tracing the patterns of God it is necessary that mothers and fathers have a comfortable and practical familiarity with them, and that they teach their children from the scriptures at every opportunity. Without the stories found in the scriptures, entry into pattern tracing becomes nearly impossible. Assuming a love for holy scriptures, let us consider five steps in pattern tracing and teaching pattern tracing to our families:

Step 1: Becoming Aware. As we read the scriptures we are guided by the Holy Ghost, the gift of which is given all who submit themselves to the Father in the ordinances of baptism and confirmation. As we familiarize ourselves and our families with scripture, the Spirit makes us aware of some holy occurrence or spiritual event that resounds through our beings. For example, we may suddenly thrill at the profound importance of Joseph Smith's First Vision, as he tells the story in Joseph Smith–History, in The Pearl of Great Price. If we are attuned, we may be led by the Spirit to see the event in our mind's eye as if for the first time, as the Spirit prompts us to discover illuminating truths that have been hovering for a time just beyond our comprehension. If pursued, these truths will enrich our spiritual lives and advance us and some members of our families (the rate and time of such discovery varies) to a new level of gospel understanding.

Step 2: Identifying the Parts of the Pattern. We study prayerfully

Joseph Smith's account of his vision and identify the ten steps which the young man followed in receiving his call to prophethood:

1. His soul hungered for divine truth
2. He was humble, brokenhearted, and contrite
3. He searched the scriptures (and "stumbled on" James 1:5–6)
4. He prayed to the Father in faith
5. He encountered satanic opposition (and was threatened with destruction)
6. He cried for help in the name of Jesus Christ
7. He was released from the grasp of the dark power
8. He was visited in person by the Father and the Son
9. He was called to serve God and told of his mission
10. He accepted the call and went forth to serve

Step 3: Discovering the Pattern As It Is Found Elsewhere in Scripture. As we study the scriptures with this pattern in mind, we begin to see similar steps in the calls of other prophets of God. We become aware that the steps Joseph Smith took toward receiving his call to his ministry are very similar to those Jesus of Nazareth took at the time of His baptism and His forty-day sojourn of trial and temptation in the wilderness of Judea. We become aware that the pattern is almost exactly replicated in the callings of Enoch, the brother of Jared, Abraham, Moses, Enos, Alma the Younger, and Paul. And when we overlay the pattern on what details we can glean about the callings of Adam, Noah, Isaiah, Jeremiah, Samuel, Malachi, Lehi, Nephi, Jacob, Peter, James, John, and Wilford Woodruff, it seems safe to assume they took similar steps before being called by the Lord to their respective ministries. And, given the need of prophets and apostles to bear *personal* witness of the Lord, we can probably assume that the prophets, seers, and revelators of all dispensations, including our present prophets, seers, and revelators, have traced this Called to Serve Pattern in their lives.

Step 4: Realizing the Pattern in Our Personal Experience and Ministries. When we overlay the Called to Serve Pattern on our own lives and, as it were, "liken all scriptures unto us, that it might be for our profit and learning" (1 Nephi 19:23), we retrace our own, similar steps that we have taken en route to our own awakening to spiritual realities and personal testimony and realize that we have been following the route of the fathers in retracing the patterns of the Father.

Step 5: Applying the Pattern. Realizing our relative positions along the spiritual route back home strengthens our faith, undergirds our confidence, and cheers our souls, attesting as it does to the close and comforting mentorship of the Holy Spirit, our Father's able ambassador. So encouraged, we not only forge ahead with greater purpose and direction, but we are able to point out the way and clarify the pattern for our spouse, our children, our family, our extended family, our neighbors, friends, and associates. We are able, as was Jesus, in teaching the multitudes, to teach "as one having authority" (Matthew 7:29)—the authority of inspired personal witness supported by the patterns of other consecrated and pattern-following lives.

There are a multitude of patterns which frame the finger of the Lord in our lives and bring His ways and means into focus. One of the patterns that has guided me in exercising personal faith first smacked me in the right eye as a young missionary. Only later did I understand that the "One Step into the Dark Pattern" recurs often in the scriptures and in our daily lives. President Harold B. Lee named it best when he taught us to "walk to the edge of the light, and perhaps a few steps into the darkness, and you will find that the light will appear and move ahead of you."[1] That step into the dark is the start-up key to an act of faith. Thus the brother of Jared prepared sixteen stones and, from the darkness of mortality but with the brightness of faith, asked, "Touch these stones, O Lord, with thy finger, and prepare them that they may shine forth in darkness" (Ether 3:4). And the Lord flooded Mahonri Moriancumer (the real name of the brother of Jared) and his people with light. It is a pattern: faith precedes the miracle, as darkness precedes dawn—just as it did when Peter forgot himself and stepped out of that ship and into the darkness to walk upon the sea (see Matthew 14:29); just as it did recently when I, as home teacher, taught the "One Step into the Dark Pattern" to a large and faithful family by blind-folding the four-year-old daughter, standing her on a table, and asking her to fall off the table into the waiting arms of her daddy. Without a moment's hesitation, and despite the obvious squea-mishness of her older brothers and sisters, the little girl stood tall and fell headlong into the darkness—where she was safely caught by her father. She had taken that step into the dark—and was duly rewarded by a glad (and relieved) home teacher.

So it was for me, when, on a rainy summer afternoon in 1958, I unwittingly traced the "One Step into the Dark Pattern" while tracting along a gravel road on a hillside above Baden, Switzerland. As we walked from home to home, I was suddenly laid low by a speck of dust in my right eye. I learned, as one who had worn brand-new contact lenses for only five days, that a mote feels like a beam. I quickly extracted the lens, cleaned and rewetted it, and prepared to reinsert it. But as I held my finger at the ready, a gust of wind suddenly swept the lens from my finger-tip: My lens was gone with the wind. I stood aghast—and virtu-ally blind, being plunged instantly into 20/600 vision in one eye, which had been miraculously corrected to 20/20 only a week earlier.

Elder Neil Reading and I began to search on hands and knees in the wet gravel, sweeping an eight-foot radius from my supposed point of loss. We searched futilely for twenty minutes. Then, half-blind and half-despairing, I suggested to my compan-ion that while we were already in position, we should pray. I rea-soned with the Lord, told him about my need to see; about our need to meet our three investigator families that evening; about my feeling that there was more to be gained by finding the lens than by my learning whatever I was to learn from the loss. As I concluded the prayer and stood up, I received one of those Joseph Smith "flashes of intelligence." It surprised me, but I reacted at once. Explaining the revealed plan to my startled com-panion, I stood on my feet in the same place I had stood earlier, squeezed out my left contact lens, and was instantly plunged into the distorted, virtual blindness of 20/600 vision. I had begun my step into the dark.

Assured that my companion was on his knees and at the ready, I put my left lens in my mouth, extracted it, and, mounting it on my finger some six inches from my face, I waited—but not for long. A slight breeze caught my left lens, and it was gone. My step into the dark was now complete. I stood stock-still, heart in throat, until Elder Reading said, "I see it. It's still in the air."

"Don't lose it," I pled, and held my breath.

"It's still up," he whispered, now ten feet away. Then, from even further away, he exclaimed, "It's starting to fall!"

"Keep your eye on it," I pled again, wringing my hands in apprehension.

"I see it! I see it!" he said. There was a long pause—of three hours or seconds—and then, "Oh my gosh! Oh my gosh!"

I braced.

"Oh my gosh," he repeated; "it's landed, and"—pause . . . pause . . . pause—". . . almost right on top of the other lens!"

"You see the other lens?" I shouted.

"Yes, it's right here!"

The darkness was flooded with light.

Unable to see a thing, I crawled over to him on hands and knees. Slowly, he planted in my palm, in order, my left and right lenses—my seer stones. I wet the lenses and, with my back to the wind and sheltered by my companion's hovering frame, I implanted them: "And there was light, and it was good." And we knelt, full of gratitude, and I thanked our God for tender and tangible mercies. We pressed on to the next house, filled with wonder at a God who knows each sparrow's fall *and* the exact whereabouts in Baden, Switzerland, of Elder Cracroft's right contact lens.

There is more. There always is, for the test of a divine pattern suggests yet another pattern. An act of divine intervention, when acknowledged as such and testified of, will, like the proverbial bread cast upon the waters, come back after many days to testify, bless, and re-bless, for it witnesses an eternally re-greening and re-blossoming truth. It is a pattern. A revelation, a divine moment will continue to enjoy the witness of the Spirit regardless of the number of times it is repeated. Think about the Joseph Smith story. Think about the story of the Crucifixion and Resurrection of Jesus Christ. Think about His appearance to the Nephite and Lamanite remnant. It is a pattern which, when recollected and recounted, testifies anew and with the same power as it carried on first telling. Christ becomes alive in us as we bear witness of holy things, in any age. So this little contact lens story has reverberated in at least three ways and surprised me each time.

The first reverberation. On the Sunday after the event, I told the contact lens experience to the members of the Baden/Wettingen Branch, over which I presided. These Latter-day Saints, who had witnessed my visual difficulties up close and shared my joy in my newfound vision, reverberated with the larger meanings of the incident: they saw it as a clear-cut instance of the intervention of the holy into the life of a missionary of God.

The second reverberation. Over the ensuing years, the Wettingen Saints had occasion to tell the story to other members of the Church in Switzerland. In July 1986, exactly twenty-eight years after this incident, I returned to Switzerland as president of the Zürich Switzerland Mission. That August, as Stake President Peter Lauener introduced Janice and me to the Bern stake conference, he surprised us: "We all have known about President Cracroft for many years," he said. "He it is, brothers and sisters, who as a young missionary here in Switzerland exercised faith and found his lost contact lens. You all recall the story from Sunday School lessons and sermons." Many in the congregation nodded in recognition.

I was dumbfounded. He turned to me and said for all to hear, "Over many years, that story has been told and retold in our meetings as an illustration of the necessary steps to faith." Only then did I fully understand that young Elder Cracroft had unwittingly cast his burden on the Lord by taking an inspired and faith-impelled step into the dark. I wondered at that young missionary's faith as I wondered if that same man, now fifty years old, still possessed that same simple faith, that willingness to take a literal and spiritual step into the darkness, to fall into his Father's arms.

The third reverberation. On January 28, 1994, two days after our twenty-five-year-old daughter and Tom Lewis's bride of one short year died suddenly, naturally, and without warning—and my wife and I were plunged headlong into the dark belly of the whale—I received a letter from a former Swiss-Austrian missionary living in Salt Lake City. He knew nothing of our recent sorrow, of course. He wrote that he had recently read my name on an article and was writing to inquire if I were the same Elder Cracroft he had known briefly in 1958, at the beginning of his mission and near the end of mine. He said he had been deeply impressed by a story I had told at a missionary conference in Zürich about losing and recovering a contact lens. He had related the incident often over the years and hoped he had told it accurately. He then repeated the story as he recalled it. Although I had not thought about or recounted the incident in several years, I was amazed that he had captured it exactly as I recollected it and as I just told it here.

The reverberation resounded loudly in my ears. In his letter I read as if for the first time my own story, and mixed tears of joy with my tears of grief. His retelling us that story now thirty-six years later, at the darkest and most despairing moment of our lives, was no coincidence. Even amidst our tears, Janice and I knew we had received a message from the Lord reminding us that He was there with us at the fall of our dear sparrow, just as He had been there with me on that long-ago Swiss hillside. Our Father was clearly reminding us that Jennifer's loss was no final loss but merely another obstacle on our salvation journey; He was reminding us that all things, including our daughter and ourselves, were in His hands; and that we should press on, confident that, as Lehi says, "All things have been done in the wisdom of him who knoweth all things" (2 Nephi 2:24). Who knows, perhaps this twice-told tale may take on yet additional lives and sound additional reverberations in the souls of others who read this witness and need encouragement to take that one step, in faith and confidence, into the darkness.

We are surrounded by the holy. We are surrounded by evidences of the hand of God. Many of these evidences, when prayerfully examined, coalesce into patterns. These patterns, tested against the witness of the holy scriptures, give us quick glimpses of the mind and will of God and testify to us of His guiding hand in our immortal course.

The holy scriptures, those divine pattern books, are the foundation from which we launch our inquiries into the world; they are "book[s] of remembrance . . . written among us, according to the pattern[s] given by the finger of God; and . . . in our own language" (Moses 6:46). The scriptures chart and direct our search for holiness in our lives and in our children's lives, and in the lives of others of our human brothers and sisters, all children of the same Father. At the core of each pattern is the reiterated message of the scriptures, as found in the pattern traced by Alma the Younger, among many others: "never, until I did cry out unto the Lord Jesus Christ for mercy," he testifies, "did I receive a remission of my sins. But behold, I did cry unto him and I did find peace to my soul" (Alma 38:8). That peace comes to you and me and to our children when we follow the pattern traced by Adam; the pattern followed by Abraham and Enoch and Noah and Isaiah and Lehi and Nephi and Enos and Alma and Jesus and Paul; and you; and the pattern your sons and daughters and their future mates and their sons and daughters will trace unto the end of time:

> Adam cried unto the Lord, and he was caught away by the Spirit of the Lord, and was carried down into the water, and was laid under the water, and was brought forth out of the water.
>
> And thus he was baptized, and the Spirit of God descended upon him, and thus he was born of the Spirit, and became quickened in the inner man.

> And he heard a voice out of heaven, saying: Thou art baptized with fire, and with the Holy Ghost. This is the record of the Father, and the Son, from henceforth and forever. (Moses 6:64–66)

This is the pattern you have followed; it is a pattern you teach your children. This is a pattern which holds in every generation—"that the Son of God hath atoned for original guilt, wherein the sins of the parents cannot be answered upon the heads of the children, for they are whole from the foundation of the world" (Moses 6:54). As the risen Lord told His disciples in the New World:

> Now this is the commandment: Repent, all ye ends of the earth, and come unto me and be baptized in my name, that ye may be sanctified by the reception of the Holy Ghost, that ye may stand spotless before me at the last day. . . .
>
> . . . this is my gospel; and ye know the things that ye must do [the patterns ye must follow] in my church; for the works which ye have seen me do [the patterns ye are to follow] that shall ye also do; for that which ye have seen me do even that shall ye do.
>
> Therefore, if ye do these things blessed are ye, for ye shall be lifted up at the last day. . . .
>
> Therefore, what manner of men ought ye to be? Verily, I say unto you, even as I am. (3 Nephi 27:20–22, 27)

In other words, "Follow my pattern and become 'even as I am.'" Parents who discern the pattern and trace its outlines in their lives are commanded "to teach [these patterns] unto your children,"

> that all men, everywhere, must repent, or they can in nowise inherit the kingdom of God, for no unclean thing can dwell there, . . . for . . . Man of Holiness is his name, and the name of his Only Begotten is the Son of Man, even Jesus Christ, . . . who shall come in the meridian of time.
>
> Therefore I give unto you a commandment, to teach these things freely unto your children, saying:

That by reason of transgression cometh the fall, which fall
bringeth death, . . . even so ye must be born again into the kingdom of heaven, of water, and of the Spirit, and be cleansed by . . .
the blood of mine Only Begotten; that ye might be sanctified from
all sin, and enjoy the words of eternal life in this world, and eternal
life in the world to come, even immortal glory;

For by the water ye keep the commandment; by the Spirit ye
are justified, and by the blood ye are sanctified. . . .

This is the plan of salvation [the gospel pattern] unto all men,
through the blood of mine Only Begotten, who shall come in the
meridian of time. (Moses 6:57–62)

Tracing the Lord's "pattern in all things" and teaching our
families to rejoice in discerning and tracing in our lives the varia-
tions on His divine patterns that are manifest all about us
becomes a rewarding and renewing spiritual discipline for any
parent and every child on the way to becoming "even as I am,"
as Christ charged (3 Nephi 27:27). All other patterns are sub-
sidiary to this grand pattern of Jesus Christ—finding ways to
remake our souls in His image. Brigham Young taught that "the
greatest mystery a man ever learned, is to know how to . . . bring
every faculty and power of the [human mind] in[to] subjection
to Jesus Christ."[2] We learn that discipline by tracing His divine
patterns, teaching these patterns to our families, and following
the patterns, together, into eternal life.

He teaches these unvarying, incremental, upward-spiraling
patterns at every opportunity and in every setting, to all men and
women who come unto Him: faith, repentance, baptism,
renewal, and—hand-in-hand with the Holy Spirit—enduring to
the end, which is finding eternal lives in His presence. En route,
we discover more and more divine patterns through following
that other grand pattern: "He that receiveth light, and contin-
ueth in God, receiveth more light; and that light groweth
brighter and brighter until the perfect day" (D&C 50:24). Let
us continue the search; let us, with our families, "seek . . . first
the kingdom of God, and his righteousness," assured that as we

do so, "all these things shall be added unto [us]" (Matthew 6:33).

NOTES

1. Harold B. Lee, as quoted in Boyd K. Packer, *The Holy Temple* (Salt Lake City: Bookcraft, 1980), p. 184.

2. Brigham Young, *Journal of Discourses,* 1:46.

CHAPTER 4

WALKING BY FAITH

John S. Tanner

BY FAITH ABRAHAM, WHEN HE WAS CALLED TO GO OUT
INTO A PLACE WHICH HE SHOULD AFTER RECEIVE FOR AN INHER-
ITANCE, OBEYED; AND HE WENT OUT, NOT KNOWING WHITHER
HE WENT.

—*HEBREWS 11:8*

DISPUTE NOT BECAUSE YE SEE NOT, FOR YE RECEIVE NO
WITNESS UNTIL AFTER THE TRIAL OF YOUR FAITH.

—*ETHER 12:6*

In this life we walk by faith, the way often lighted before us but one step at a time. This is the common lot of all those who sojourn in tabernacles of clay removed from our heavenly home. As Paul writes of mortality: "whilst we are at home in the body, we are absent from the Lord" and hence, "we walk by faith, not by sight" (2 Corinthians 5:6–7). To walk by faith, one step at a time, has been a family theme from the very first days of our marriage. In fact, it has united the generations of my family since the early days of the Church, as it unites every disciple in the family of God across all dispensations. All must journey through mortality "by faith"—"as strangers and pilgrims on the earth" (Hebrews 11:13). All must endure "the trial of [their] faith."

This is the testimony of Paul and Moroni in parallel chapters on faith, Hebrews 11 and Ether 12, which catalogue the courage

---

John S. Tanner received his Ph.D. from the University of California, Berkeley. His specialties are Renaissance and religious literature. He has published widely in these areas as well as written essays and even a hymn for LDS publications. Having completed a six-year term as associate academic vice president, he is currently a professor and department chair of English at BYU. He and his wife, Susan Winder Tanner, are the parents of five children.

of the faithful. Paul celebrates Old Testament figures who "by faith" overcame every obstacle and "obtained promises," even though they "received not the promise" in this life (Hebrews 11:33, 39). He lists such worthies as Abel, Enoch, Noah, Abraham, Moses, and many others—including women—who "wrought righteousness" and "of whom the world was not worthy" (Hebrews 11: 33, 38). Likewise, Moroni praises Book of Mormon heroes who "by faith" wrought miracles and obtained promises from God (see Ether 12:17, 22). He cites Alma, Amulek, Ammon, the brother prophets Nephi and Lehi, the brother of Jared, and "even all they who wrought miracles . . . by faith" (Ether 12:16).

Over the years, my wife, Susan, and I have cherished these scriptures and taught them to our children. Our family has taken courage from Abraham who obediently left his home "not knowing whither he went" to "sojourn" as a "stranger" [foreigner] in the land God promised him, "and died in faith, not having received the promises, but having seen them afar off . . . and embraced them" (Hebrews 11:8, 9, 13). And we have found hope in Moroni's words that often the Lord does not supply full understanding "until after the trial of your faith." In fact, we have come to feel that the trial of faith informs virtually every other trial we face, standing as an ordeal within the ordeal. For almost every hardship requires that we suffer not only it, but also the ordeal of uncertainty occasioned by it.

Consider, for example, the ordeal of starvation faced by the Saints who first came to the Salt Lake Valley. According to one eyewitness, Parley P. Pratt said that the pioneers who endured that first terrible winter in the Salt Lake Valley suffered more from fear than from actual hunger.[1] Think about that. Remember how hungry the Saints were: "The people tried eating crows, thistle tops, bark, roots, Sego Lily bulbs—anything that might offer nutriment or fill the empty stomach."[2] Yet they suffered most from fear. For "the valley was new," explains Elder Pratt, "ne[i]ther was it proven that grain could be raised."[3] Uncertainty can be more chilling than winter, doubt more gnawing than hunger, and tempests of the mind more fearful than the raging storm. As Shakespeare's King Lear remarks: "The tempest in my mind / Doth from my senses take all feeling else / Save what beats there" (3.4.12–14).

In a similar vein, Alexander Solzhenitsyn describes the surprising reaction of people rounded up by the Soviet secret police after they had been in hiding for many years: "Sometimes the principal emotion of the person arrested is relief and even *happiness!*" After all, Solzhenitsyn explains, there is a kind of exhaustion that is "worse than any kind of arrest." He illustrates this point by citing the example of a priest who, having eluded capture for eight years, "suffered so painfully from this harried life that when he was finally arrested in 1942 he sang hymns of praise to God."[4]

Not knowing *when* or *if* or *how* an affliction will end is often more taxing than the affliction itself. This ordeal within the ordeal defines a perennial human predicament. Thus all ages echo the ancient cry, "How long, O Lord, how long!"[5] We do not plead to know "how long" only because we wish to escape our woes, but also because we feel that we could brave almost any distress better if we knew the bounds of its duration—and because in this knowledge lies also the assurance that our sorrows are bounded.

I think, for example, of my single adult children. How much more patiently and profitably could they bear being unmarried if they knew that in three years they would marry a good person—or, alternatively, that they would never marry. It is not the condition of being single but the uncertainty of that condition that can seem unendurable. Likewise, I think of my newly married daughter and son-in-law. How much less stress would they face if they knew where and when he would complete law school, or how her pregnancy will turn out. Bar exams and labor pains describe only the outward content of their trials; beneath these circumstances lies the deeper, spiritual trial of faith—that their lives are in God's hands. This is so for all of us, in almost all our trials.

But we wish it were not so. In periods of prolonged duress,

we yearn for the Lord to carry us to a mountaintop, as he did Moses, and there reveal in detail the course of our lives (see Moses 1). We want to know the beginning from the end. Instead, the Lord leads us step by step through the wilderness, like Nephi or Abraham, "not knowing beforehand" what we should do (see 1 Nephi 4:6) or whither we should go (see Hebrews 11:8). In this life, "we see through a glass, darkly," longing for the day when we shall see God "face to face" and know as we are known (1 Corinthians 13:12). To live on this side of the veil is to learn to "walk by faith, not by sight" (2 Corinthians 5:7), and to "feel after" the Lord (see Acts 17:27; D&C 101:8) as He lights our way home, one step at a time.

My parents taught me the scriptural lesson that we walk by faith in part by instilling in me a love for the hymn "Lead, Kindly Light" by John Henry Newman. Susan and I have tried to do the same. We have taken this hymn into our hearts and our hearth, teaching it to our children until now it is a family favorite. Newman penned the lyrics aboard ship on the way home to England from Italy. He was not only homesick and sea-sick but, more important, sick with longing for divine guidance. Though he didn't yet know it, he was also about to take the first faltering steps of spiritual pilgrimage that ultimately would lead him, and many who followed, to another church. In these circumstances, Newman wrote:

> Lead, kindly Light, amid th' encircling gloom;
> Lead thou me on!
> The night is dark, and I am far from home,
> Lead thou me on!
> Keep thou my feet; I do not ask to see
> The distant scene—one step enough for me.[6]

This final phrase has become a watchword for our family.

"One step enough." How often have Susan and I repeated these words to our children and taken comfort ourselves in this phrase. Yet even with these words on our lips, we still tread gingerly into a future that sometimes seems so precarious and into which we can often see safe footing for only one small step ahead, craving precisely that which we profess not to ask for: namely, to see the distant scene. For, as most everybody, we yearn for certainty and would avoid risk, if we could. Suspense makes us, well, nervous. Susan's the kind of reader who, when the suspense becomes too intense, skips to the end of the novel to see how it will turn out. I am the kind of sports fan who sometimes opts to watch a close game on replay, *after* I know the outcome. And several of our children can scarcely abide the anxiety of a suspenseful movie.

The dramas of our own lives, however, are not available to us on video or in novels. We can neither read ahead, nor fast forward the tape, nor walk out of the room. Our tribulations unfold in real time. This being so, the only way out, alas, is through. Hence, we must endure not only our hardships but the ordeal of anxiety within the ordeal. We must learn to live on promises, walking by faith and receiving witnesses about the wisdom of our path only in retrospect.

As our children have grown, the example of Abraham, especially as it is recounted in Hebrews 11, has become increasingly important in our family circle. We remember that the faithful are called the "children of Abraham" (Galatians 3:7). To walk by faith is to tread in Abraham's footsteps. We have taught our children that, in an eternal sense, all the faithful are called, like Abraham, to become pilgrims. "By faith" Abraham left not only his home in Ur of the Chaldees, but the security of settled city life itself, to become a nomad. Well writes the nomadic Abraham of his journey from Mesopotamia to Canaan: "Therefore, eternity was our covering and our rock and our salvation, as we journeyed from Haran . . . to come to the land of Canaan" (Abraham 2:16). The heirs of Abraham know that God is the best and only true security.

We have taught our children that Abraham did not cease to be a nomad after he arrived in the promised land. Rather, even in Canaan he dwelt "in tabernacles" (i.e., tents), "as in a strange [i.e., foreign] country." While his nephew Lot chose to live "in the cities" on the "well watered" plain of Jordan (see Genesis 13:10–12)—and reaped the consequence of that choice—Abraham dwelt not in cities. "For he looked for a city which hath foundations, whose builder and maker is God" (Hebrews 11:10). The heirs of Abraham know that "here have we no continuing city, but we seek one to come" (Hebrews 13:14).

We have taught our children that as Abram wandered through Canaan, he was promised the land over and over again. Yet when Sarah died, Abraham had to buy the cave of Machpelah in which to bury her. How poignant are Abraham's words to the sons of Heth, from whom he purchased the cave: "I am a stranger and sojourner with you: give me possession of a burying-place with you, that I may bury my dead out of my sight" (Genesis 23:4).

The land was Abraham's by covenant, yet near the end of his life he did not own even a plot of ground sufficient to inter Sarah's body. Later, Abraham was buried in this same cave, the only property he ever owned in Canaan! (see Genesis 25:9–10). No wonder Stephen says that the Lord gave Abraham "none inheritance" in Canaan, "no, not so much as to set his foot on," but promised only that he *would* give Abraham the land "for a possession, and to his seed after him, when as yet he had no child" (Acts 7:5). The heirs of Abraham know that walking by faith means holding fast to promises though they seem "afar off" (Hebrews 11:13), for "the Lord is not slack concerning his promise, as some men count slackness" (2 Peter 3:9).

We have taught our children that Abraham spent all his days living on promises—not only with respect to the promised land but also with respect to a promised posterity. With what could seem like cruel irony, the Lord repeatedly pledged Abram posterity as numerous as the dust of the earth and the stars of heaven, and changed his name to Abraham, "father of a multitude." Yet all the while Abraham had no promised heir; all the while he and Sarah were growing older.

At last, of course, Isaac was born. Then the God of Abraham, with what must have seemed cruel irony, required the sacrifice of the very child through whom the prophecies that Abraham's seed would become "a great and mighty nation" were to be fulfilled (Genesis 18:18). How is it that Abraham "staggered not at the promise of God through unbelief" (Romans 4:20), but "believed in the Lord," who "counted it to him for righteousness!" (Genesis 15:6). The heirs of Abraham know that our journey home will appear checkered with ironies; yet we must not stagger through unbelief, but be believing.

Finally, we have taught our children how to read Abraham's trials, as well as those of the other prophets. We have tried to teach them that to read scripture only from the comfortable retrospective of history is to risk distorting their trials. For the participants did not enjoy the luxury of historical knowledge about how things would turn out. As we read the scriptures, therefore, we should remember their fear and trembling.[7] We should flee with Abram from Haran, not knowing whither we go, with eternity as our only rock; wander with Abram in Canaan, living on increasingly incredible promises about possessing the land and a great posterity; journey with Abraham to Mt. Moriah, prepare the altar for Isaac, and lift the knife. In short, we should become "contemporaneous"[8] with Abraham in his trials. Only then will we understand why Abraham is called the father to the faithful, the model for all those who, like him, die in faith, "not having received the promises, but having seen them afar off, and were persuaded of them, and embraced them, and confessed that they were strangers and pilgrims on the earth. For they that say such things declare plainly that they seek a country. . . . A better country, that is, an heavenly: wherefore God is not ashamed to be called their God: for he hath prepared for them a city" (Hebrews 11:13–14, 16).

We have also tried to liken these scriptures unto ourselves (see 1 Nephi 19:23) by sharing with our children their heritage of Abrahamic faith. Among the stories we have shared is that of John Tanner, their fourth great-grandfather and the first Tanner to join the Church. Shortly after the original John Tanner was converted, he felt prompted to sell his beautiful farm in Lake George, New York, and move to Kirtland—not knowing he was led there by the Spirit to help rescue the Church from debt. The Prophet Joseph had prayed Father Tanner to Kirtland. Several more times John and his family left everything to follow the Saints—from Kirtland to Jackson, from Jackson to Nauvoo, from Nauvoo to Salt Lake. With each move Father Tanner and his family became poorer; with each dislocation they had to start anew. But because eternity was their rock, they left their progeny a legacy of faith more precious than gold.

We have also shared the story of my paternal grandparents, William and Clara. They lost two grocery stores in the Depression. Their sole remaining possession of value was a home. Then came a mission call to their oldest son, my Uncle Dick, who assumed it was impossible for him to serve. Of course you'll go, his parents told him. They sold their home and moved into an attic apartment. Friends were very critical and, from a practical point of view, their criticism was justified, for my grandparents lived many more years but never again owned a home of their own. Yet they gave their sons, including my father, something more valuable than an estate. They gave them an Abrahamic legacy of faith.

Likewise, my own parents have walked with a faith of truly biblical proportions. Despite a world war, long years of school, and never knowing financial stability, my parents got the education and had the family they felt the Lord expected of them. Mom walked across the stage to receive her diploma when she was expecting her first child. Six of us were born by the time Dad received his Ph.D. Seven more children were still to come, this despite constant economic uncertainty from my father's self-employment. Yet they sent ten children on missions, often with more than one in the field at once, and made sure that all thirteen graduated from college. Now, my folks worked very hard for this. We, too, were expected to sacrifice: to save for missions, to put ourselves through college. But beside hard work, my parents exhibited even more heroic faith. They were faithful to the Abrahamic legacy of their parents and grandparents.

Thus, for example, my father responded much as had his father when I was called in for my pre-mission interview at a time when it would have been highly imprudent for me to accept a mission call. My brother was already in the field, I had limited funds, and Dad was overextended, having had to borrow some of my mission savings to meet family expenses. Yet I'll never forget his advice to me: "John, if you receive a call from the Lord, you go. A way will be provided." And a way was provided.

In these stories it's easy—too easy—to see the faith and miss the fear. But you can't miss the fear and trembling when it's your own history. We have also shared with our children our own experience with walking by faith, in which the witness awaited the trial of faith. In 1974, when I was a senior at BYU, the job market for English professors was desperately tight and predicted to get much worse. It seemed only prudent to do something practical, like apply to law school. But as I wrote Duke Law School the obligatory essay on "Why I Want to Be an Attorney When I Grow Up," it struck me, with the force of revelation, that I did *not* want to be a lawyer. I wanted to teach, preferably Renaissance literature. What's more, I felt the Lord wanted me to teach. So I tore up my essay and applied instead to graduate school in English. The distant scene seemed so uncertain; all the forecasts said not to follow the less trodden path I was taking. Yet the little light that illuminated my feet seemed to point to graduate school. A way was soon opened up for me to go to UC, Berkeley, but only one step ahead.

At about the same time that I tore up my law school application I became engaged to Susan. I was painfully aware that all I had to offer my bride were long, impoverished years in graduate school and then . . . the prospect of no employment in my chosen field. I had only enough money for one quarter's tuition. Plus, Susan and I also both wanted children and felt this was our first priority when we married. I was inexpressibly happy about my marriage, but also very anxious about the uncertain future. So I sought a blessing from my father. I received, like Abraham, promises—cherished, treasured promises, but nothing you could take to the loan officer at the bank: "The Lord is mindful of your desires," I was told. "He knows your concerns and approves this marriage; the way will be opened to complete your education through means you cannot now conceive."

With these promises in hand, we set off for Berkeley. "Eternity was our covering and our rock and our salvation." Six long years and four children later I had my degree and, miraculously, a job in my field. Way after way had indeed been opened before us. For example, a housesitting job that we thought would last only a few months became, through the generosity of saintly Jim and Roma Sabine, three years of rent-free housing. I was able to find full-time night-watchman jobs at which I could study all night and go to school all day. And even when we were making only sixty dollars a month on my early-morning seminary salary, we paid our tithing and, somehow, made ends meet. The Lord was on our right hand and our left, lighting our way one step at a time.

My faith, however, was not so strong as Abraham's. Many times I doubted the future. Oh, I could meet the present distress, but was anxious about the future. How often would I lament: "What am I doing to myself and my family! There are no jobs in English. I can't complete a Ph.D. anyway. After all, I almost flunked freshman English. I can't write. I can't type. I can't even spell. What madness to think *I* can do a dissertation!" Still the years stretched on. Still anxiety enveloped my faith. My former roommates completed law school, took real jobs, bought cars and homes. My best friend went on to clerk at the Supreme Court. Meanwhile, I pulled weeds at the Oakland Temple and worried about completing a seemingly interminable degree. Yet I persisted, borrowing generously from the faith of my wife, whose unshakable conviction that teaching was my vocation kept us walking down an uncertain path, one step at a time.

How much more courageously and cheerfully could I have lived on promises had my faith been as strong as hers. I am reminded of the ending of John Bunyan's *The Pilgrim's Progress,* which portrays Christian and Hopeful crossing the river of death. There "was no bridge to go over," Bunyan writes, and "the river was very deep." The two pilgrims begin to despair, for there is no way across except through. Then they learn this truth: "you shall find it [the river] deeper or shallower, as you believe in the King of the place."[9] Susan generally finds the river shallower than I. Both of us, however, have to wade by faith.

Now we see our children enduring similar trials of faith. And as we once delighted in their learning to walk, we now find joy in their learning to walk by faith. As we watch them pray, fast, study the scriptures, and pore over patriarchal blessings, we know that they are learning to make the Lord a lamp unto their feet (see Psalm 119:105) about matters large and small—from the minutia of what to major in, to the more momentous decisions of mission and marriage.

So our family sojourns through mortality by faith, as "pilgrims and strangers," "children of Abraham," heaven bound. Soon we will be joined by our first grandchild, born on the cusp of a new millennium. This child will inherit a world very different from that of its ancestors. Yet no matter how far advanced materially or technologically its generation is from theirs, he or she will still need to learn to walk with the faith of Abraham. For each generation starts in the same place with respect to life's eternally significant tasks, and each discovers that faith is a "task for a whole lifetime."[10] Faith is not only a first principle, but a foundation principle of righteousness. We learn about faith from infancy, but we never grow out of it on this side of the veil. Thus we expect our grandchildren to be taught faith from the scriptures, hymns, and family stories recounted herein, which have become so dear to us as a family. But we also expect them to learn that their parents, grandparents, and great-grandparents are still learning to walk by faith. Each new day calls that we "fresh courage take."[11] Each new trial also tries our faith in some new and poignant way. Each new setback forces us to rely on promises and throws us to our knees. And often the way seems confused and dark before us, reminding us that in this life "we walk by faith, not by sight."

NOTES

1. See *A Mormon Chronicle: The Diaries of John D. Lee,* as quoted by Eugene England in *Brother Brigham* (Salt Lake City: Bookcraft, 1980), p. 146.

2. Leonard Arrington, *Great Basin Kingdom* (Lincoln: University of Nebraska Press, 1959), p. 49.

3. *Brother Brigham,* p. 146.

4. Alexander Solzhenitsyn, *The Gulag Archipelago, 1918–1956; An Experiment in Literary Investigation, I–II,* trans. Thomas P. Whitney (New York: Harper & Row, 1974), pp. 14–15.

5. See, for example: Psalm 13:1–2, 35:17, 89:46; Habakkuk 1:2; Alma 14:26; D&C 121:2–3.

6. John Henry Newman, *Hymns,* no. 97.

7. For a discussion of this with reference to Abraham, see Soren Kierkegaard, *Fear and Trembling,* trans. Alastair Hannay (Harmondsworth, England: Penguin Books, 1985).

8. See Soren Kierkegaard, *Training in Christianity,* trans. Walter Lowrie, (Princeton: Princeton University Press, 1967), 66 ff.

9. John Bunyan, *The Pilgrim's Progress,* ed. N. H. Keeble (New York: Oxford University Press, 1984), p. 128.

10. *Fear and Trembling,* p. 42. Cf. 145–46. See also George Herbert's poem "The Agony," which notes how some truths, like love and sin, are deeper than philosophy and science can measure.

11. William Clayton, "Come, Come, Ye Saints," *Hymns,* no. 30.

CHAPTER 5

Moroni, a Singular Saint
Marilyn Arnold

We all knew it was coming sometime, the death of my elderly parents after a lengthy period of decline. Their passing was especially momentous for me, a single person living alone, because they were the center of my family life. My tenderest feelings were for them, and my deepest anxieties were over their physical mountains and emotional valleys. Parents are important to all their children, but when parents die, a person without spouse or children is perhaps more bereft of family than married siblings.

I think that the loss of Mother and Dad is probably somewhat different for my brothers than it is for me. They experienced the same anguish, the same worry and care over the last several years that I did. Like me, they invested much emotional and physical energy into seeing our beloved parents "through," as we said. And they ached, as I did, over the almost terrifying downslide and then the passing of those two anchors in our lives. But when my father's funeral concluded, and he was buried

Marilyn Arnold is a professor emeritus of English at Brigham Young University and holds a Ph.D. in American literature from the University of Wisconsin at Madison. She was the founding director of the Center for the Study of Christian Values in Literature at BYU and has served as dean of Graduate Studies at the same institution. A resident of St. George, Utah, she is the author of Sweet Is the Word, Pure Love, Desert Song, *and* Sands of Pardon.

beside Mother, each of my brothers returned to his daily life with his wife and his own family circle of children and grandchildren. I returned to an empty condominium in Southern Utah, a vast desert inside me as well as out.

Since my father's second bout with cancer ten years ago, he had been much changed. What had begun as deteriorating physical strength and somewhat unreliable memory for recent events soon became feebleness of both body and mind. My mother, who had been nearly blind for many years, suffered a stroke four years ago, a misfortune that left her body greatly reduced but her remarkable mind still intact. What we hadn't expected was that the two of them would die this summer, a month and a day apart. Even as I draft this essay, not yet two months after my father's passing, the weeks and days prior to their deaths are vivid in my memory; and their faces keep surfacing to crowd other images from my mind.

Still, in the sorrow of losing them, I rejoice for their release from spent bodies and for their blessed reunion as whole beings after just a month of separation. Among friends and family, especially, I am able to put grieving aside for certain stretches of time and become absorbed in matters of life rather than in matters of death. I am at last able to work again, and I am learning how to sleep once more and how to play. But for me, the separation is already longer than the month my parents were apart from each other, and it could well continue for many years.

As a rule, I don't mind living alone, being a family of one. Much of the work I do is, by necessity, solitary work. Two or more people can't really sit at the same computer keyboard and punch out words together. And my affection for the out-of-doors has always kept me happily active and in love with life. In fact, when away from the desert, I hunger for the solitude of sand and red rock. Coming home after two deaths and two funerals, however, was different. I had never felt so helpless as in the face of my parents' suffering. I had never before seen dying up close. Processing all that, plus losing the steadying influence and the security of parents at the end of every drive north, made coming home hurt just a little. But it also brought the second Moroni, the guardian of the priceless records, very close, and I found myself turning to him for both consolation and inspiration. Whatever I was feeling, whatever I had suffered—and even what my parents had suffered, I realized—could not begin to compare with what he felt and suffered. Maybe part of his mission was to stand as a model of courage and faith for all of us, including those who define family in the singular.

I have loved Moroni a long time. Like the first Moroni, that fiery champion of liberty, and Jacob and Ammon too, he has been something of a scriptural brother to me—human and dear as well as faithful and strong. I admire Lehi, Nephi, Benjamin, Alma, and others immensely, but they are more like fathers than brothers to me. Perhaps I know them less as people than as leaders. Although the record reveals some of their human qualities, their humanness tends to be overshadowed by the forcefulness of their leadership and the magnitude of their accomplishments.

Moroni, on the other hand, had no one to lead but himself for the last thirty or so years of his life. With the help of the Lord he made it on his own, one solitary human being. Of late, I have found myself turning to Moroni repeatedly and ignoring the tag in Mosiah that marks my progress on this reading. And I prize the book of Mosiah. These days, however, my study copy seems always to open at the eighth chapter of Mormon, where Moroni declares his intent to complete his father's record.

There, he tells of the last great battles in which all the Nephites who didn't defect to their enemies were killed. Any who escaped after the wars "were hunted by the Lamanites, until they were all destroyed" (v. 2), all, that is, but Moroni. For me, with the obvious exception of the account of the Savior's crucifixion, there is no more heartbreaking passage in scripture than verse three of Mormon 8: "And my father also was killed by them, and I even remain alone to write the sad tale of the destruction of my people. But behold, they are gone, and I fulfill the commandment of my father [to complete the record according to Mormon's instructions]. And whether they will slay me, I know not."

As is evident from the passages cited, the opening verses of chapter eight are heavy with sorrow. How could they be otherwise? Can any of us begin to imagine the soul-shattering experience of witnessing the moral and then the physical ruin of an entire nation, *our* nation, a whole civilization? Can we even envision ourselves as the sole survivor of a family, a neighborhood, a community, a country? Moroni stood there, very likely wounded himself, face to face with the reality of mother, father, wife, possibly brothers and sisters, children, cousins, and friends gone, annihilated in horrific slaughter. Homes, churches, schools, government buildings, businesses—gone also.

Moroni, indeed, knows something about loss, about death, about suffering, about aloneness. His words, especially words such as "alone" and "gone," resonate in my mind, and I feel his pain. I doubt that anyone on the face of the earth has ever, before or since, been so totally stripped of human association and sympathy. We who are single would do well to consider this when we are tempted to count other's blessings instead of our own. The only people left in Moroni's world were bloodthirsty murderers who craved his life. The Lord could well have mentioned Moroni as well as Job in responding to the Prophet Joseph's agony in Doctrine and Covenants section 121.

The reader can hear the despair in Moroni's words as he contemplates his predicament and mourns his loss: "Therefore I will write and hide up the records in the earth; and whither I go it mattereth not" (Mormon 8:4). Even adding to the record seems beyond him at this moment of wreckage and grief. I would write the purpose of the record, as my father has done, he says, "if I had room upon the plates, but I have not; and ore I have none, for I am alone." As if still trying to comprehend the tragedy, Moroni says again that his father was "slain in battle," as were "all [his] kinsfolk," leaving him to face his hazardous destiny alone. "I have not friends nor whither to go," he laments, "and how long the Lord will suffer that I may live I know not" (v. 5). Furthermore, the war continues among the remaining Lamanites, "and the whole face of this land is one continual round of murder and bloodshed; and no one knoweth the end of the war" (v. 8).

Not only was Moroni alone, but he was a fugitive, a man in perpetual danger. Even after the Jaredite abridgement was completed, possibly months or years later, the peril remained: "I had supposed not to have written more," he says, "but I have not as yet perished; and I make not myself known to the Lamanites lest they should destroy me" (Moroni 1:1).

Those of us who comprise one-person "families" can find in Moroni someone who also lived alone, but under circumstances scarcely comparable, or even conceivable, to modern readers, single or married. Most single people of my acquaintance have family members in other dwellings in other places. They enjoy comfortable homes and stocked pantries, good friends, supportive neighbors and ward members, police protection, medical assistance, and so on. And so as we take consolation from Moroni's life and words, we would do well also to take instruction from his extraordinary example and his soul-stirring discourses and admonitions.

Most obvious, perhaps, is his lesson in endurance. Giving new meaning to the term, Moroni did more than endure; he grew in strength. Living, as he had to, by his wits and by the support of the Lord, he transcended his feelings of aloneness and defeat and survived for three decades in a hostile land. He not only survived, he carried out his father's injunction, under what must have been extreme hardship, to complete the record and secure it for future generations. It would appear, too, that the three translated Nephite disciples, though they had "ministered unto" Moroni and his father Mormon, were not "suffer[ed] . . . to remain" when wickedness swallowed the whole land. Moroni adds that "whether they be upon the face of the land no man knoweth" (Mormon 8:10). He lacked even their comfort.

Given the devastation that encompassed him, and the seeming hopelessness of his situation, it would have been easy for Moroni to have given up, to have languished in self-pity, or perhaps even to have let himself be killed or to have taken his own life. Trials of any kind are a test of our mettle, and we can choose to grow from them, as Moroni did, or we can choose to be destroyed by them. My mother, in all her infirmity, was much like Moroni. Both Moroni and mother chose to get on with life and duty, and grew in the process. To all appearances, in the years following her stroke mother was not left alone in a desolate waste roamed by enemies. But in another sense, she was. With my father's mind largely gone, she not only had to take herself through a wilderness of personal disability, but she also had to take him through. And she had to do it with failed vision, failed physical strength, a failing heart, and limbs that no longer worked properly. I have learned from watching her that nothing can be more lonely than living twenty-four hours a day with the unperceiving, completely dependent, and thus largely unsympathetic, shell of one's beloved lifemate.

Mother also lived daily with her enemies—pain, fear, frustration, helplessness, discouragement, embarrassment, dependence, indignity. And she prevailed. And she grew spiritually. Like Moroni, she never gave up, and she never stopped praying, both entreating the Lord for strength and thanking him for His tender care. There were times when she wanted to quit, when it seemed she could not go on, when she longed to go to sleep and not wake up. But somehow, as Moroni must have done, she stirred herself and kept on.

In the years before the stroke, when through a special eyeglass she learned to focus what peripheral vision remained in one eye, Mother would hold a text against that eyeglass and make out a few letters at a time. Painstakingly putting letters together, she constructed words as she moved the page across her face. Reading in that manner, she completed the Book of Mormon four times. It became a dear companion to her and a great source of strength. I watched her faith deepen, and we talked together of scripture and doctrine in ways we never had before. After the stroke destroyed most of her remaining peripheral vision, she listened to the scriptures on tape, rejoicing in them, feasting on them. Eventually, she could no longer operate the tape machine, but she clung tenaciously to what she had gained. She was a light to me then, and she remains so in my memory. Mother was a Moroni person.

That Moroni grew in his seemingly endless years of aloneness and danger is evident. I think of his first sorrowful utterances, and then the powerful admonitions and doctrinal messages that follow them. I think of his times of self-doubt with regard to his writing ability, and the way in which he moved beyond self-doubt to confidence in the record, the Lord, and himself. But those anxious times bring him closer to me, for I, too, have doubted myself and felt inadequate to a task. From him, in those moments, I learn the lesson of humility. I also learned it from my mother as she increasingly had to rely on others, increasingly had to relinquish her temporal life to the hands of both loved ones and strangers. And self-doubt troubled her as it troubled Moroni. There was a time when she blamed her continuing blindness on what she supposed then was her lack of sufficient faith to be healed.

So worried was Moroni about his writing and that of his predecessors, and so important did he deem the writing for the convincing of his readers, that he interrupted his work on the book of Ether and its teachings to report a conversation he had with the Lord on the matter. In speaking with the Lord, Moroni addresses a theme he had mentioned before, his concern that human flaws might compromise the record's credibility. "The Gentiles," he pleads, "will mock at these things, because of our weakness in writing; for Lord thou has made us mighty in words by faith, but thou has not made us mighty in writing" (Ether 12:23). We speak, he tells the Lord, by the power of the Holy Ghost, but "thou hast made us that we could write but little." He does not soon drop the subject, either. We are not "mighty in writing like unto the brother of Jared," who wrote so mightily that it overpowered a "man to read" his words, he says. You have made our spoken words so powerful, Moroni continues, "that we cannot write them; wherefore, when we write we behold our weakness, and stumble because of the placing of our words; and I fear lest the Gentiles shall mock at our words" (Ether 12:24–25).

Even though to the modern reader Moroni seems amply gifted in writing, the Lord does not reprimand him for his fears, nor does the Lord dismiss them out of hand. Rather, he answers Moroni's humility with gentle assurances that mortals are given weaknesses to make them humble, adding that his "grace is sufficient for all men that humble themselves before me . . . and have faith in me." The Lord comforts Moroni by affirming that He "will make weak things become strong unto them" (Ether 12:27).

One can almost measure Moroni's growth by comparing his first farewell statement in Ether with his last in his own book. The former comes at the conclusion of Ether 12, cited above, in which the Lord allays Moroni's fears about the record. In the final four verses of that chapter, Moroni bids farewell to "the Gentiles" and to "my brethren whom I love," bearing testimony that he has seen and spoken with Jesus. He urges his readers to seek Jesus and desires that the Holy Ghost will abide with them (see vv. 38–39, 41). At the same time, he is apologetic for his "weakness in writing" (v. 40). While Moroni's farewell in Ether is not weak by any means, neither does it match the vitality and triumph of his farewell in Moroni 10: "And now I bid unto all, farewell. I soon go to rest in the paradise of God, until my spirit and body shall again reunite, and I am brought forth triumphant through the air, to meet you before the pleasing bar of the great Jehovah, the Eternal Judge of both quick and dead. Amen" (Moroni 10:34).

Maybe the inner growth in my mother was not obvious to most people, who would have seen mainly her diminished frame and her loss of strength and agility, but it was obvious to me. And it was my great blessing to share a good many spiritual moments with her, talking and reading. I saw her face glow as she spoke with wonder and gratitude of the Book of Mormon, a treasure she had come to love with all her heart. I heard her prayers and felt the power of her deepening testimony. I saw her thrill to the words of scripture and to the words of living prophets, on tape and radio. Those things are available to everyone, regardless of family size.

I also marvelled at my ninety-three-year-old father, who was unable to follow a newscast or a ballgame on television, but who listened intently, and seemed to understand, whenever conference was broadcast or scriptures were played on tape. I came to know that his spirit apprehended what his mind could not grasp. That was confirmed when I sat next to him at mother's funeral service and heard him sing, in his sweet, flawless tenor, all verses of both congregational hymns. I can only think that he, too, somehow grew spiritually in his particular kind of trial. I know now, also, that the trials of my parents, by becoming my trials as well as theirs, strengthened me spiritually, although at the time those struggles seemed to be undermining my physical strength and testing my emotional stamina to the limit. More reason for me to turn again to Moroni.

There is also the matter of faith. If Mother had lost faith, she would not have survived to carry my father through the last several years of their lives. Nor could she have endured, with him, the radical cancer treatments, the frequent serious falls, and the slipping mind. And she, too, loved Moroni. He was a model and a hero to both of us. What if he had succumbed to circumstances? we asked each other and ourselves. What if he had stopped relying on the Lord and living by the Spirit? Mother felt at times as though she carried the world on her frail shoulders, trying to keep a household operating, determined not to move Dad to unfamiliar surroundings so long as she had an ounce of strength. Moroni must have felt that way, too. Everything depended on him, the eternal future of Jew and Gentile alike. And he was just one mortal being. If he had faltered, barring divine intervention, the record could well have been destroyed by his enemies. His enduring faith is another great lesson for every individual.

Still another lesson to be learned from the life of Moroni is perhaps less apparent than lessons of faith and endurance, but it is of the utmost importance. As I struggle to be a better person, to stop disappointing the Lord, Moroni is a bright example of the pure love of Christ in action. In his first farewell to the latter-day reader alluded to above, he speaks of "my brethren whom I love" (Ether 12:38). These "brethren" of whom he speaks so lovingly, for whom he repeatedly expresses grave concern, and for whom (through their descendants) he is completing and protecting the priceless record, are the same people who have brutally slain his father and all his loved ones, the same who have demolished the Nephite cities, the same who have denied their God, the same who would kill him if they caught him, the same who would destroy the record if they found it. In his words we hear echoes of Christ's injunction to "love your enemies, bless them that curse you, do good to them that hate you" (Matthew 5:44). We also hear Christ's incredible words uttered on the cross: "Father, forgive them; for they know not what they do" (Luke 23:34). Few mortals, I suspect, have come nearer to being truly Christlike than Moroni. In him is love unfeigned, forgiveness seventy times seven, selflessness that shames our overindulgent lives.

Moroni's whole concern is for persons other than himself, including those of us blessed beyond measure to have the record in our lives. A particularly valuable lesson for the person living alone. He warns against the sins that will plague our times, and he delivers a powerful discourse on faith (see Ether 12:6-22) even as he frets over his supposed rhetorical shortcomings. We should make no mistake; Moroni's anxiety over his writing ability has nothing to do with ego and everything to do with eternal life for God's children. He knows what the record has cost his forebearers, he knows it is vital to the salvation of the House of Israel, and he wants desperately for it to be well received. In everything he is selfless. How few of us manage to devote our lives to high purposes outside ourselves, while Moroni lived and endured solely for the good of others, and to fulfill his father's and his Lord's commandments.

There is another way, too, in which Moroni has touched my life. At this particular juncture, when my feelings toward my parents are especially tender, I find solace in the sweet relationship between Moroni and his father. When Moroni speaks of his father's labors with the record and his father's death, it is clear that this father and son greatly loved each other. Their mutual love is even more evident in the two letters from Mormon to his son that Moroni chose to include in the record (see Moroni 8 and 9). Moroni could have abridged those letters, or excerpted them, engraving only the doctrinal and instructional matters on the plates, but he does not. The letters appear in their entirety, and they teach us truths that extend beyond canonical theology. Mormon's opening words in the first letter define the relationship between himself and his son, modeling for us the kinds of expressions that should pass between parent and child:

> My beloved son, Moroni, I rejoice exceedingly that your Lord Jesus Christ hath been mindful of you, and hath called you to his ministry, and to his holy work.
>
> I am mindful of you always in my prayers, continually praying unto God the Father in the name of his Holy Child, Jesus, that he, through his infinite goodness and grace, will keep you through the endurance of faith on his name to the end. (Moroni 8:2–3)

Throughout the letters, Mormon addresses Moroni as "my son," and "my beloved son," and he expresses concern for his son's well-being and safety in the dangerous times in which they live: "But behold, my son, I recommend thee unto God, and I trust in Christ that thou wilt be saved; and I pray unto God that he will spare thy life" (Moroni 9:22). Mormon's closing words to Moroni in the second letter are especially touching, perhaps because he realizes that he might not see his son again in mortality (see Moroni 9:24). These words are in the form of a father's blessing:

> My son, be faithful in Christ; and may not the things which I have written grieve thee, to weigh thee down unto death; but may Christ lift thee up, and may his sufferings and death, and the show-

ing his body unto our fathers, and his mercy and long-suffering, and the hope of his glory and of eternal life, rest in your mind forever.

And may the grace of God the Father, whose throne is high in the heavens, and our Lord Jesus Christ, who sitteth on the right hand of his power, until all things shall become subject unto him, be, and abide with you forever. Amen (Moroni 9:25–26)

I know with certainty—because sometimes I was there—that words to this effect were continually in my parents' hearts and on their lips for their children. Only recently have I fully realized the immeasurable blessing of being reared in a home, modest though it most assuredly was, where love was spoken and demonstrated in a hundred ways daily. Moroni's world collapsed around him, but he did not collapse. I am convinced that the enduring love of Mormon for his son, his righteous expectations of that son, and his earnest prayers in behalf of that son, played a major role in sustaining Moroni through tribulations that he does not even bother to describe. The fact that Moroni returned to his father's discourses and letters, writing some of them into the record, suggests that the memory and words of his father were part of the spiritual armor that saw him through.

Those writings have served such a purpose for me, too, and I express everlasting gratitude for them, and for all I have learned from my dear brother Moroni, a single and singular saint.

CHAPTER 6

BOOK OF MORMON MARATHON
Carlos E. Asay

It was a cold and dreary December day in Bad Vilbel, West Germany, as my wife and I sat in our cozy apartment and discussed plans for the new year. The year 1987 was drawing to a close and 1988 fast approaching.

Our thoughts first turned to home and members of the family living thousands of miles away. We missed the children and grandchildren and wondered how each was faring without the immediate presence and smothering attentions of loving grandparents.

Next, we began thinking about our Church assignments, which included responsibilities for the work in the British Isles, Scandinavia, Europe, Africa, and the Middle East. We discussed conference schedules, mission tours, and other details of a year full of heavy demands upon our time and energies. And, we wondered what we might do to magnify our callings and to bless the lives of the stream of Saints and sinners that we would meet in the coming twelve months.

A recent letter from Church headquarters in Salt Lake City

Carlos E. Asay, an emeritus member of the First Quorum of the Seventy is currently serving as president of the Salt Lake Temple. He and his wife, Colleen, are the parents of six sons and two daughters. He is the author of In the Lord's Service, The Seven M's of Missionary Service, *and* The Road to Somewhere.

reminded us that the Church curriculum for adults in 1988 would focus study upon the Book of Mormon. Reflecting upon that course of study, I said to my wife, "Don't you think that we should get a head start on that program?" I recalled having heard of people, particularly new converts, who had read the Book of Mormon cover-to-cover within a few days or even hours. A case in point was the experience of Parley P. Pratt, one of the early Church leaders and one of the great missionaries of all time. In reference to his introduction to the book, he wrote: "I opened it with eagerness, and read its title page. I then read the testimony of several witnesses in relation to the manner of its being found and translated. After this I commenced its contents by course. I read all day; eating was a burden, I had no desire for food; sleep was a burden when the night came, for I preferred reading to sleep."[1]

My wife noted that we were midway through the month. And, in her sly, nudging way challenged, "If you want to be half the man Brother Parley was, and if you want to do what he did, you have the luxury of fifteen whole days to read the Book of Mormon cover-to-cover before the year's end." The challenge was too enticing to turn aside. My wife had struck a nerve in my conscience, as she is so adept at doing, and, as you might say, "goaded me with gracious goodness to do something very right."

In my methodical style, I divided the number of pages in the Book of Mormon (531) by fifteen. This simple mathematical procedure gave me a quotient of thirty-five and one-half (the number of pages that I would be required to read each day in order to reach my goal.).

I next prepared a reading chart, plotting the days and the chapters included in each thirty-five and one-half page segment. And, like Elder Pratt, "I commenced its contents by course." Some days I read the planned segment and more. Other days, when demands upon my time were greater, I read less than the prescribed number of pages.

My enthusiasm for the project grew page by page. Reading was no burden at all, and I found myself jealously guarding the time allocated for my daily visits with Nephi, Jacob, Alma, Helaman, and the other spiritual giants mentioned in the Nephite record. I reached the point where I relished picking up the book and loathing the time when I had to put it down.

On the last day of the month, my wife and I were en route to the Middle East on Church business. Just as the landing gear of our Air Jordan flight lowered into place before touchdown in Damascus, Syria, I closed my Book of Mormon, leaned back in my seat and exclaimed aloud, "I did it!" Passengers close by were startled by my outburst—my cry of victory—and wondered what I had done. But, my wife knew. She smiled and planted a kiss on my cheek.

At the same time, my eternal companion glanced at her wristwatch, noting that it was exactly 2100 hours, and said, "Why don't you read the book again in January? After all, you have a three hour head start on the new month." Then, prodding me even further she observed, "It will be much easier for you to have thirty-one days to do what you have done in fifteen."

Once again, the challenge was too intriguing to ignore. I knew within my heart that the compacted reading of the Book of Mormon had provided me with a type of pentecostal experience. It had lifted me to a higher spiritual level. It had given me a companionship with men of God of a bygone day who shared with me a fifteen-day pilgrimage through inspired print. It had stirred my soul and whetted my appetite for more. And, though I had read the book many times before, I was now beginning to really understand and appreciate the words of the Prophet Joseph Smith, who said: "I told the brethren that the Book of Mormon was the most correct of any book on earth, and the keystone of our religion, and a man would get nearer to God by abiding by its precepts, than by any other book" (Introduction to the Book of Mormon).

My rather concentrated reading had, indeed, brought me closer to God in many ways. Scriptures from the Book of Mormon were surfacing more frequently in my sermons. Words and phrases from the book were popping up in my conversations. I found myself applying teachings from the book in counseling priesthood leaders and others. Subconsciously, I was doing what Nephi suggested: I was likening the scriptures to me and those around me "that it might be for our profit and learning" (1 Nephi 19:23).

Consequently, I resolved that I would read the Book of Mormon twelve more times in 1988. I knew, however, that each monthly excursion had to be more than simply a coverage of the text. I knew that I had to dig into the book and "post-hole" specific doctrines.

Survey reading, or reading for coverage, does have its virtues. It provides an overall view of the subject at hand. But, the serious student of the scriptures does more than skim the surface. He identifies a certain topic or subject and "post-holes" it by cross-referencing, consulting related sources, and digging deeply for greater understandings. In the process, he searches the scriptures diligently, ponders their meanings, and prays about them so that he "might know (really know) the word of God" (Alma 17:2; see also Moroni 10:3–5).

In a sense, my survey reading of the Book of Mormon had taken me out of the plains of Moab and to the top of Pisgah, where the Lord provided me a panoramic view of God's dealings with the ancient inhabitants of the Americas from the first book of Nephi all the way to Moroni (see Deuteronomy 34:1–4). The perspective gained of the book was exhilarating, yet not enough. Now it was appropriate for me to descend the mount and go among the people and probe deeply into their lives. I needed to walk among the Nephites, sit at the feet of inspired prophets, and meet with them in their homes and in their streets and upon their hills and in their temples and in their synagogues (see Alma 26:29).

Since the Book of Mormon is another testament or witness of Jesus Christ, I determined to mark all references to the Savior in the conduct of my January reading. I noted that there were nearly twelve pages of references to Jesus Christ listed in the index of the Book of Mormon. I noted that the invitation "Come unto Christ" was one of the recurring themes or golden threads woven into the fabric of the text. I noted that Jesus of Nazareth was truly the focal point of worship among the ancients of America. Each contributor to the record, it seemed, had labored diligently to write and to persuade readers to believe in Christ and to be reconciled to God (see 2 Nephi 25:23–26).

January's "post-holing" effort caused my understanding of the Savior to increase measurably. I came to know Him as I had never known Him before. Additionally, it deepened my love for the Holy One of Israel. I speak of a love that stirs within one's heart a higher resolve to live better and serve more devotedly. His life, His mission, His Atonement, and all else associated with His saving role became indelibly inscribed in my heart. Christ was now "post-holed" in my soul.

I selected as my in-depth study for February another golden thread that runs through the Book of Mormon account. It is the promise as old as Lehi (600 B.C.) and as recent as Moroni (420 A.D.), which reads: "Inasmuch as you shall keep my commandments ye shall prosper in the land; but inasmuch as ye will not keep my commandments ye shall be cut off from my presence" (2 Nephi 1:20).

I discovered in my reading and "post-holing" effort that God's promise to the Nephites was validated time and time again. Individuals were blessed when obedient to God's commandments. Groups of people, even nations, were blessed during times of righteousness. However, both individuals and groups fell upon hard times when they rebelled against divine laws and teachings. Little wonder that I found myself urging my family members and others to live for the promise and to write their own blessings by the way they lived and served. Having "post-holed" this promise in my own heart, I wanted others to know that it had never been rescinded and is just as applicable today as it was anciently.

A third golden thread of the Book of Mormon occupied my attention in March. It is the warning to avoid hardness of heart and blindness of mind. Only one of the many references to this warning that I highlighted in my book reads as follows: "And thus they have been called to this holy calling on account of their faith, while others would reject the Spirit of God on account of the hardness of their hearts and blindness of their minds, while, if it had not been for this they might have had as great privilege as their brethren" (Alma 13:4).

After "post-holing" this timeless warning, I wrote:

> Much like the sightless man who cautiously makes his way down the street tapping his cane to identify the hazards that lie ahead, the person "blind of mind" stumbles awkwardly through life. Every step is tentative; each roadblock is almost insurmountable; and progress is painfully slow at best. Of such people it is said they "have eyes to see, and see not"; "Their eyes cannot see afar off"; they "shall see, and shall not perceive." . . .
>
> You need to realize that hardness of heart is a gradual, subtle illness and not a massive heart attack that comes with little or no warning. It begins with the breaking of a single law. It grows layer by layer as more and more commandments are flaunted and as one thus becomes less and less able to distinguish between right and wrong. Then, as time lapses and rebellion increases, the once gentle and feeling heart becomes an impenetrable flint. No one is more hardened in character than he who has, without repenting, transgressed the laws of God, the laws of loving parents, and the laws of nature.[2]

Subjects "post-holed" in April, May, June, and July were the first principles and ordinances of the gospel: *faith* in the Lord Jesus Christ; *repentance; baptism* by immersion for the remission of sins; and the laying on of hands for the gift of the *Holy Ghost* (see the fourth article of faith).

I read and reread Alma's insightful discourse on faith, wherein he likened the word of God to a seed (see Alma 32). This discourse, in company with Ether's teachings about faith, was most enlightening and helped me understand why hope and faith "maketh an anchor to the souls of men" (Ether 12:4).

I reveled in the accounts of men who rose from the darkest abyss of sin and climbed into the realms of the righteous through repentance. Alma the Younger's transformation from rebel to prophet says much about the principle of progress called repentance (see Mosiah 27). And, who can ever forget the Lamanite king who was willing to give away all his sins and forsake his kingdom to know God? (see Alma 22:15–18).

Much is said in the Book of Mormon about the ordinance of baptism. "Post-holing" this subject brings into marvelous light reasons why the Savior was baptized (see 2 Nephi 31), specific baptismal covenants (see Mosiah 18:8–10), the abominable practice of infant baptism (see Moroni 8), and many other truths relative to the gateway into the kingdom of God.

It is difficult to pinpoint only two or three highlights from the Book of Mormon pertaining to the Holy Ghost. Nevertheless, the writings about angels and the Holy Ghost (see 2 Nephi 32), and the promise given to the truth-seeking reader must be mentioned (Moroni 10:3–5). In the process of "post-holing" this subject, I found myself courting this sacred influence with greater intent and purer motive.

My "post-holing" topics in succeeding months proceeded as follows: August—references to the fiery flying serpent account; September—references to missionary service and methods of proselyting; October—references to war (justification, strategy, prisoners, and so on); November—references to the anti-Christs and other enemies of righteousness; and December—references to the source of power experienced by mighty leaders (revelation, prophecy, testimony, priesthood, or holy order).

When my Book of Mormon marathon was completed, I enjoyed a marvelous feeling of accomplishment. At no time did I tire or hit the proverbial wall in my reading. Each hour, each day, and each month with book in hand I was transported back in time and space and permitted to mingle with a chosen people who inhabited a land of promise. Their trials and hardships became my trials and hardships. Their lessons learned became my lessons learned. In the end, it was made obvious to me why the record was preserved and allowed to come forth in my day as another testament of Christ.

At year's end, my wife commented, "Carlos, you are not the same." My response was, "Thank God for that." I did not want to be the same because my reading for coverage and "post-holing" of Book of Mormon eternal truths had sunk deeply into my soul and made a difference. Now, I desired, with Lehi, "that my family [and my readers] might [also] partake."

NOTES

1. Parley P. Pratt, *Autobiography of Parley Parker Pratt*, ed. Parley P. Pratt (Salt Lake City: Deseret Book, 1938), p. 37.

2. Carlos E. Asay, *The Road to Somewhere* (Salt Lake City: Bookcraft, 1994), pp. 10–11.

CHAPTER 7

HOUSEHOLD SCRIPTURES: THE ART OF BUILDING WITH THE WORD

Kristen D. Randle

I am a spiritual pygmy. Not to cast any aspersion whatsoever on the pygmies who are, I am certain, just as generally admirable as any other group of people; it is stature I am addressing, of which—physically and spiritually—I have little.

I say this as baldly as I do in hopes that my kindred spirits—those as generally chagrinned to be Knocking on the Door as I am—will hear and understand that they are not alone in the feeling.

I do not come from a long line of LDS pioneers, nor do I have the dignity or benefit of having been, myself, a new convert to the Church. I am a child of converts, of intelligent, hard-working, determined, and practical-minded folk. It would have been easy to depend on their testimonies if I were the kind of person who is comfortable letting somebody else drive my bus for me; I am not that kind of person. Couple this restless inde-

---

Kristen D. Randle, daughter of honorable parents, is a long-term wife and the mother of four fine children. She is a graduate of BYU and presently resides in Utah. She has also lived in Los Angeles, Missouri, New York, and Texas. She has written seven novels, including The Only Alien on the Planet, *which received an ALA Best Book award and was named the Michigan Library Association Book of the Year in 1996.*

pendence with a dearth of spiritual talent, and you have a mighty busy squirrel in an awfully small wheel.

The scriptures are not easy for me. Not that I can't read them. That, at least, I can do. But I am enough of a word person to know that language is at best imprecise. No, I will step back further and say that even the act of trying to define the smallest part of the universe with a word is a desperately temporal effort to pin truth to a safe wall. In both the complexity of Truth and the utter simplicity of it there are attributes that are incomprehensible to our minds—bound as we are by this earthly condition—and as many words as we paste over our lack of understanding, it is lack of understanding, still.

Thus, reading the scriptures has to be more of a mystical experience than an intellectual one—allowing the Spirit to use the words in ways that surpass our greatest hopes for the usefulness of language. And there's my problem; being spiritually deaf, dumb and blind, I do my best. But I still don't do very well.

These confessions out of the way, I will tell you that, in thinking about all this, I find that I am a little shocked—though not surprised—at how thoroughly the scriptures have been woven into the fabric of our little family, at how thoroughly they have been woven into me.

In fact, I am convinced that a family cannot achieve the kind of depth of love and understanding we Latter-day Saints seek without constant use (do not read *use* as simply *reading*) of the scriptures, that the counsel and wisdom of the prophets and the very words of the Lord can get us through some very tough situations, especially when diligent use of these scriptures is coupled with humility, prayer, and love. I am further convinced that every effort should be made to connect very young children with scriptures through the stories and aphorisms of these books, the theory being that a child brought up this way will not tend to depart from it. I've got to figure that my testimony of this begins with my own kid-feelings, and I know that my experience as a parent has only made it more sure.

I don't know when I started loving the scriptures, but I do

know that it started with a puppy love that had very little to do with Truth or Philosophy. My first church book, given to me at baptism, was a white New Testament, leather-covered and embossed with gold lettering. I could zip it closed, or run my hands over its pebbly surface, or sift through the delicate pages until I came up hard against the pictures, some of which were pretty scary. It was thumb indexed in the most fascinating way. Not only did having it make me feel very adult, but that book also gave me plenty to do when I was bored in Sunday School. My first Book of Mormon was the brown one with the gold Moroni on it. No thumb indexing. No onion-skin pages. No zipper. But the chunkiness of it charmed me.

Just owning these books made them mine in a very intrinsic sort of way. And so, in light of those old feelings, Guy and I have been careful to give each child a full set of scriptures. We make it a "Great Baptism Gift"—a sort of rites-of-passage thing given with ceremony. These are not the expensive versions; vinyl covers that look like leather can make a kid feel sufficiently adult. I have known adults who have brought themselves closer to the community of Saints by the simple expediency of carrying a personal set of scriptures, and thus feeling spiritually grown-up themselves.

But it is in the opening of these books that many people become discouraged. The language is admittedly tough reading, especially if you haven't been brought up to love reading in general. My dad used to read to us at bedtime—fairy tales, short stories, children's books. In this way, he made language part of the warmth of home, and wove words into the concept I was building of myself. When he read *The Land of Promise* series to us, he mixed the sweet comfort of Daddy-at-bedtime with stories from the Book of Mormon, giving those stories the benefit of the full range of his voice, infusing them with a drama both human and immediate.

My family moved to Texas in my last year of high school, and there I happened to strike up an acquaintance with my new friends' Church of Christ youth minister. Instead of sitting through study hall, I'd trot over across the street to this minister's church, meaning to study the New Testament with him. He was a smart guy—he'd studied Greek and Hebrew, and he gave me insight into the language of the scriptures that I'd never gotten anywhere else. For one thing, he taught me that the verb from which our word "baptize" comes actually means "submerge," by showing me a Greek account of a sea battle in which one ship was said to have "baptized" another. "I don't think they meant 'sprinkled,'" he grinned.

Of course, the scripture study inevitably turned into a gentle and amiable doctrinal debate. Every night, I got myself ready for these meetings, eventually reading the New Testament right through from beginning to end for the first time in my life. I discovered the concept of tithing there and felt like I was meeting an old friend in an unexpected place. I found phrases in Paul's letters to the Hebrews that made me laugh out loud, they seemed so real and human.

I expect the fact that I was reading this stuff on my own and having to explain it to somebody who didn't share all of my perspectives was the beginning of my spiritual independence. I was reading to a point, not just doing a nominal fifteen minutes a day or chapter a night. And because of that, I began to push at the meaning burgeoning behind the veil of words.

A couple of years later, I took a Doctrine and Covenants class from Richard O. Cowan at BYU. He taught modern revelation as though he were lecturing law. I was reading Chiam Potok at the same time I was taking this class, and I remember that Brother Cowan's class made me feel like I was studying the Talmud. I would pore over each section, taking notes on tiny pieces of yellow paper, wresting meaning out of each passage of scripture as if it were something you could hold in your hand, something you could hold up to the light. I can remember sitting in the library, doing this reading and being so excited, so suffused with meaning, I had to stand up to get my breath. Such a feeling that was—my book carefully read, carefully marked.

Again, remembering the strength of that feeling, Guy and I

encourage our kids to mark their own scriptures—another very adult thing, to have permission to write in books. "If you hear or read something that's cool," we tell them, "underline it so you can find it again." We've even been known to buy those translucent illustration things you paste into your scriptures, thereby letting the kids become a part of their own books.

During those college years, I began to understand the impact scripture reading had on my process of thought. I was a little amazed to realize that I tended to see the world not as an opaque reality, but as a translucent metaphor. I sensed shadows of meaning behind every physical fact, seeing things and circumstances as lessons, types. All the world was a parable to me, and so everything was significant—an encouragement or a reproach, a map, a type and a shadow. I understood the Pantheists, then— at least I understood them as they'd been explained to me—why they believed the world we live in to be a second book of scripture.

At this time, I had a most personal experience with the scriptures.

One day, my sister, Keven, also then a student at the "Y," but about three years behind me, called to see if she could borrow my car. It was *my* car, a little yellow Volkswagen bug I'd bought from my dad. And I told her no. I didn't even think twice about it. What's more, I felt indignant that she should have asked. I still don't understand how I managed to do it, but in that snotty state of mind, I dropped right down on the couch, picked up my Book of Mormon and righteously snapped it open—directly to Mosiah 4:16: "And also, ye yourselves will succor those that stand in need of your succor; ye will administer of your substance unto him that standeth in need; and ye will not suffer that the beggar putteth up his petition to you in vain, and turn him out to perish." I felt as if I'd been taken by the scruff of the neck and shaken. Not that Keven would have *perished* without my car . . .

There will be those who, reading this, will be sure that there was no coincidence involved here; I am not now and will never be sure that it wasn't a coincidence. I am not a strong believer in letting the scriptures fall open for answers—this smacks too much of soothsaying for me. But I am not about to bind the Lord's hands, either. However it happened, that scripture entered into my mind with a fierceness I have never forgotten, and stands in the background like a subroutine in my operating system, all because I had read it at a particularly expedient moment. I called my sister back and lent her the car.

One day soon after that, when I didn't seem to be getting any of the things I wanted in my life and all kinds of terrible, frustrating things were happening to me, I finally broke down and wailed. My friend, Roger Hoffman, having heard the whole lament through, asked me thoughtfully, "Have you been reading your scriptures?" My doctor now asks me, "Have you been taking your vitamins?" in exactly the same tone of voice.

"Yes," I told Roger—and this was the outrage, of course, that I had been doing all the right stuff and ending up feeling so lonely and lost anyway—"every night."

"Ah," he said, nodding. "I see. To prepare you for the hard night ahead."

I hiccuped and frowned and narrowed my eyes at him. It had never occurred to me that it might make a difference *when* you did the righteous things. And suddenly, all these little bits of understanding seemed to line up: meaning, understanding, thought, Spirit—all tools to be used by the calm mind with intelligence and wisdom. Deliberately used.

I am writing about all of this as a preface: you build a family with the tools you've collected along the way. The Lord doesn't give any of us a free new toolkit at the moment of marriage, or at the moment of conception, or even at the birth of a child. Through all of this, we have to use the kit we've been putting together all our lives long, adding to it as we go. My middle daughter's favorite Primary song, she told me many years ago, was "Search, Blunder and Pray." And so I have done.

Here I'm going to say another thing: a father who has been on a mission and knows the scriptures, who reads them, quotes them and carries them is an important thing. But to my eye, it falls to the mother to do the basic, sturdy construction of family fabric—to the mother who stays home and interacts with her children on a regular, fundamental basis. Such mothers do the lion's share of the weaving. And so the scriptures, if they are going to be part of the goodly garment, have to start in the mother's hands.

When my children were babies, I saved my scripture reading for nursing. I'd hold the baby in the crook of my arm with the chunky little Book of Mormon open in my hand. In the way of babies, especially comfortable ones, one hand would eventually go exploring, only to find that interesting book. Without missing a minor suck, each baby in its turn over the years would open one eye, pat the book, look it over, mess with the pages. It was important, I thought, to associate the scriptures with being thoroughly fed.

When the children were little, I wrote several albums of children's music, little songs meant to illustrate stories and principles. My kids used to listen to these as they went to sleep at night. Later, we graduated to real art—to Peace Mountain's delightful *Scripture Scouts* series, a children's reader's theater offering. These recordings are deceptively simple, written with understanding, wit, and love and performed by children. I could listen to them very cheerfully, lying beside a sick or worried child. What I like about this series is the fact that the writers don't put words in the mouths of prophets, while they do require the child to do some painless mental work. (I do not, on the other hand, care for animated videos of scriptures stories; I don't want my kid carrying around some animator's concept of Nephi in his heart.) These simple introductions to the scriptures built a context through which I could meet the kids' understanding, Truth *a lá* kid. This is called groundwork. Alongside all this, we were teaching our children to love reading. These things seem to me now an echo of my father's nightly bedtime reading.

Further, we've had fits of organized scripture reading over the years, with the glowing hope that we'd finish the Book of Mormon all together some time before the youngest child leaves on his mission. Each person gets a chance to read out loud, to feel the shape of those fine words in the mouth; the kids seem to love their chance to shine—especially because we make such a big deal about how well they're doing. We stop between scriptures to talk about the words and the ideas so that nobody gets lost—again, giving each child a chance to hazard his interpretation of the scripture.

But in actual, mundane family practice, Guy and I use the scriptures much the way my mother used them: with excellent aim. You load the scriptures into your own head, keep your finger on the trigger, and keep an eye out for likely targets.

My mom's favorite was "Do unto others . . . ," perhaps because I gave her ample opportunity to use it. My sister, a cute, sweet, wonderful little kid, had ruined my chances to be an only child; I had to hit her. When she began to wail, my mom would come out swinging—"DO UNTO OTHERS . . . and just what, exactly, do you think THAT might mean?"

Not a good question. "It means," I'd tell her, tongue solidly in cheek, "that Keven has just shown me how she wants to be treated, and so if I'm going to be polite, I have to treat her that way. Which is the way I just treated her."

I use the same scripture my mother did, but you couldn't pay me to ask her question. Instead, I follow the scripture up with a different query: "If so-and-so had done this very thing to *you*, how would you be feeling right now?" There is no way around that question; leading questions are better than open-ended ones. There is a limit to the freethinking you want your children to do. I collect the kids' answers and usually end up yelling at each of them in a cheerfully egalitarian manner.

I have to tell you that I don't have any faith-promoting stories about how a certain scripture once helped us through a specific problem, or how a specific experience with the scriptures has changed our lives. Rather, the scriptures just sort of crop up at odd times, influencing our thinking and our choices.

Some of my favorite scriptures have hung on our refrigerator so long, their index cards are dead yellow: Alma 37:36–41:

Yea, and cry unto God for all thy support; yea, let all thy doings be unto the Lord, and whithersoever thou goest let it be in the Lord; yea, let all thy thoughts be directed unto the Lord; yea, let the affections of thy heart be placed upon the Lord forever.

Counsel with the Lord in all thy doings, and he will direct thee for good; yea, when thou liest down at night, lie down unto the Lord, that he may watch over you in your sleep; and when thou risest in the morning let thy heart be full of thanks unto God; and if ye do these things, ye shall be lifted up at the last day . . .

Nevertheless, because those miracles were working by small means it did show unto them marvelous works. They were slothful, and forgot to exercise their faith and diligence and then those marvelous works ceased, and they did not progress in their journey.

and Mosiah 10:11:

Now the Lamanites knew nothing concerning the Lord, not the strength of the Lord, therefore they depended upon their own strength. Yet they were a strong people, as to the strength of men.

Which is another point, I guess—put the scriptures right at eye level so that every time somebody goes for a cheese sandwich, that person can't help reading a passage or two. You have to be careful, though, because people tend to stop seeing what's always there; shifting the location of the scriptures every couple of days would probably be wise, so that people will think "Hey, what's this?" and read the scripture again before they figure out it's just the same old thing.

Alma 34, especially the part from verses 20 through 27 has comforted me when I otherwise might have felt unworthy, guilty for trying to draw upon the Lord for the mundane protection of our children and of our temporal life:

Cry unto him when ye are in your fields, yea, over all your flocks.

Cry unto him in your houses, yea, over all your household, both morning, mid-day, and evening . . . .

Cry unto him over the crops of your fields, that ye may prosper in them.

Cry over the flocks of your fields, that they may increase. . . .

Yea, and when you do not cry unto the Lord, let your hearts
be full, drawn out in prayer unto him continually for your welfare,
and also for the welfare of those who are around you.

Alma 5:22 has cleared the way for me to live with irony, following Moroni's example and subjugating the uncivilized in my
own home: "while Moroni was thus breaking down the wars and
contentions among his own people, and subjecting them to
peace and civilization."

The end of all this is that the only thing my oldest son, a
cheery, bouncing boy of seventeen, asked for this last birthday
was a real leather Bible (he's got the triple, which costs something less and so is easier to get), something he can take on his
mission and keep all of his life—a book he can mark up and read
and love and use when he is a father himself. This is not because
he is a sanctimoniously serious person, but because he has been
brought up with scriptures and understands that they are important in the nuts-and-bolts business of his life.

Perhaps it is because I feel so desperately inadequate to pilot
these children through a world that is at once so fiercely beautiful,
and so terribly, humanly obscure and dangerous that I value these
scriptures. I may not be able to reach beyond the veil for understanding, but these words have been there, and so I offer them to
my children as a shining, brilliant treasure—as though I hold the
Urim and Thummim in my own hands—to lend strength to the
bones of my children's characters and to serve as balm to sometimes sore souls.

We live in a house made of scriptures. They are in our walls
and ceiling, our foundation and the roof under which we rest.
Their words and wisdom are the weave that holds the house
together, the windows through which we see all the world. They
are the conduit through which so much of our fresh air comes.
Somehow, this has happened without my noticing. Maybe it's

the way we invite the words in for supper, the way we include them in our offhand discussions. Such a quiet, simple thing to have proven so essential.

CHAPTER 8

HARMONY FROM APPARENT CONTRADICTIONS

Richard Neitzel Holzapfel

Shortly before my call to serve a full-time proselytizing mission at nineteen years of age, I found myself seriously searching the scriptures for the first time in my life. And while I was acquainted with them through my earlier Church activity and as a natural consequence of living in a country imbued with Judeo-Christian tradition, they seemed for the most part to be nothing more than stories of dead people written on dead trees.

Beginning with the six-month period before my mission labors and continuing through the next two years of service among the people in Italian-speaking Switzerland and Italy itself, the Lord breathed life into the pages of the scriptures as I opened my heart and mind to His words.

I experienced a real baptism of fire, and I was consumed by the desire to read the scriptures often and take every chance to

Richard Neitzel Holzapfel is an assistant professor of Church History and Doctrine at Brigham Young University. He is the author of numerous articles in the Ensign, Utah State Historical Quarterly, Western Historical Quarterly, *and* BYU Studies, *and has written nineteen books, including* Sisters at the Well: Women and the Life and Teachings of Jesus *(co-authored with his wife, Jeni);* Every Stone a Sermon; Old Mormon Nauvoo; Utah, a Journey of Discovery; *and* A History of Utah County.

do so. There was joy in my heart when I read completely all four standard works for the first time just before entering the mission field. The message of salvation contained therein was so glorious it seemed as though it needed to be shouted from the rooftops.

Leaving college, earning the money to serve for two years, and rearranging my priorities was anything but a sacrifice. Once in the mission field I continued to love the scriptures and found great satisfaction in detailed study and reading. I eventually had somewhat of a reputation for being a serious student of the scriptures in the mission field.

And while I began to quote chapter and verse readily and knew many of the inspired interpretations by Church leaders, I was still very much immature when it came to understanding the deeper meanings within them. After those early days of basking in the light of the scriptures I began to see that they not only answered the great questions of life (Who am I? Where did I come from? Where am I going?), but they contained answers to immediate and personal concerns in my life. This realization came in a powerful and personal way and more significantly, it changed my life with my family.

Finishing graduate school and beginning a family was a challenging time. Like many people living in the fast lane I was so busy that, quite frankly, it was nearly impossible to get into any trouble. Blocks of time during the days and evenings were filled with so many obligations and activities that my choices were generally between competing good things to do. I could visit this family in my Church assignment, I could go to this fireside, I could go to the temple, I could work on my personal history, I could visit family members in a nearby community, or I could work extra hard on a project at Church or at my place of employment.

Days flowed into weeks, weeks into months, and months into years. I felt that I was beating the drum, but it still seemed that I was not living after the manner of happiness mentioned in the Book of Mormon. And while I was busily engaged in a good cause, I often felt that my goals and commitments were opposed to each other even though those goals were all good and highly sought after by faithful Latter-day Saints.

As I considered my calling as a father and husband, my assignment as a bishop, my employment responsibilities, and my educational goals, I knew that all the bases were not being covered as well as they should have been. In particular I felt a pull between the time I was spending with my family and the time I spent in Church service. In some ways, both assignments seemed at odds with one another since my assignment as bishop was not in my own ward, but over a singles' ward, thus making it very difficult to spend time with my family. Added to this was the challenge of fulfilling my employer's expectations and my own educational pursuits to improve my employment opportunities and provide for my family.

I was active in the Church and living as I should so I could live with my family forever, I worked hard at my employment to provide for my family's temporal needs, and I went to school to make a better life for myself and my family. Yet, it was my family that always seemed to be getting the least amount of my time. It reminded me of university students who work so they can go to school, but miss class because they have to work!

One story reveals the irony involved in my life at this time. My wife received new visiting teachers in our home ward. After several months of visiting, one of the sisters took courage and asked my wife if I was a non-member or simply inactive in the Church. Her surprised response tells it all: "No! No! He is too active!"

When told of the incident I laughed with my wife, but there was something to it all. I knew and used the *quality* versus *quantity* argument, justifying myself countless times. Having accepted this argument at face value I told myself that it was the *quality* that mattered, not the *quantity*. As a result I substituted so-called *quality* experiences with my family in place of the quantity time they really needed and deserved.

Something happened that changed all of that. The time was right for the scriptures to become a vehicle to change my life in a significant way. I may never know the combination of events that brought me to this point, but a series of small things happened that led me to ask some important questions of the scriptures about my philosophy of life.

The first event was on a business trip. I struggle to be occupied on airplanes so I generally grab as many magazines as I can to read during the flight. I do not remember the name of the magazine, the author, or the title of the article I read, but it began the process that led me to the scriptures.

The author of the article discussed the issue of quality versus quantity and used an expensive dinner at an exclusive restaurant as an analogy to open the issue for his readers. He wrote something to this effect: "Imagine going to a famous restaurant to enjoy the chef's special main entree, one that he is renowned for and one that has made him a celebrity. You already know the bill will be very expensive, but you are willing to pay it because of the reputation of the restaurant and the expectation of an enjoyable gastronomical feast. When the main course is served the waiter brings a special silver server. Your mouth begins to water and the silver cover hiding the entree's smell only heightens your expectation. When the cover is lifted you find a very tiny serving. You can hardly believe your eyes. You complain to the waiter only to be met with the now famous response: 'It's the quality not the quantity that matters!'"

The analogy hit me right between the eyes, and I imagined those most important to me feeling as the customer in the above analogy felt—angry, frustrated, and cheated. What was I to do? What could I cut out of my life in order to feel good about both quality and quantity issues with my family, yet still be a good employee, a good student, and a good servant in the kingdom?

Here the tire hit the road; the scriptures were no longer simple vehicles to tell me about the great plan of happiness, or a means of giving me knowledge about the Lord's dealings among His children. I needed to know something very important and precise about myself and my life right then as I proceeded faster and faster down the road of life.

As I searched for a personal answer it happened—I noticed something I had not noticed before. At least, I had never applied it to my life before as I did on this occasion.

I was reading the gospels of Mark and Luke and 3 Nephi at the time, a happy combination in light of my discovery. As I was thinking about my dilemma and wondering how I could fulfill all my assignments at Church, work, and school without short-changing any of them—especially my family—I began to see how the New Testament portrayed Jesus Christ's mortal work as a mission not only to large groups, but also to individuals.

The Gospel narratives indicate that in many cases there was direct physical contact between Jesus and individuals as He ministered among the people. For example, when He healed Peter's mother-in-law of a fever, Jesus "*touched* her hand" (Matthew 8:15; emphasis added; see also Mark 1:30–31; Luke 4:38–39); Jesus again "put forth his hand, and *touched*" a man with leprosy to make him whole (Matthew 8:3; emphasis added); and He touched the eyes of two blind men as he healed them (see Matthew 9:27–31). He healed deafness and a speech impediment when He put his fingers "into" a man's ears (see Mark 7:32–37); He "put his hands upon" a blind man (Mark 8:23); He healed a demonic child when He "took him by the hand and lifted him up" (Mark 9:27; see also Matthew 17:14–21; Luke 9:37–43); the Savior healed Jarius' daughter when He "took her by the hand" and raised her from the dead (Matthew 9:25; see also Mark 5:35–42; Luke 8:49–56).

According to Mark and Luke, Jesus often healed not merely by touching the individual but through a more formal laying on of hands (see Mark 5:23; Luke 4:40), and He enjoined the disciples to do the same (see Mark 16:18). Healing was also often conveyed through this laying on of hands in the post-Resurrection Church (see, for example, Acts 9:12, 17, 28:8). And Jesus also blessed children by laying hands on them (see Mark 10:13–16).

As I picked up the Book of Mormon to read during this same period I turned to 3 Nephi, sometimes referred to as the "fifth Gospel" in LDS scholarly circles. It describes Christ's post-Resurrection ministry to the Nephites in terms similar to those used in the four New Testament Gospels. It emphasizes the individual experiences of the Nephite people with the resurrected Messiah, noting their direct physical contact with Him as well as His laying on of hands as the symbolic act of transmitting authority and power. In addition, the use of the word *minister* in various forms is used in connection with these experiences. In his introduction to the appearance narrative Mormon states: "Behold, I will show unto you that the people . . . did have great favors shown unto them, and great blessings poured out upon their heads, insomuch that soon after the ascension of Christ into heaven he did truly manifest himself unto them—showing his body unto them, and *ministering* unto them; and an account of his *ministry* shall be given hereafter" (3 Nephi 10:18–19; emphasis added).

When Christ appeared to the ancient inhabitants of America, He invited them to "thrust your hands into my side, and also that ye may feel the prints of the nails in my hands and in my feet, that ye may know that I am the God of Israel, and the God of the whole earth, and have been slain for the sins of the world" (3 Nephi 11:14). All the people gathered at the temple in Bountiful "went forth, and thrust their hands into his side, and did feel the prints of the nails in his hands and in his feet" (v. 15), and when they had brought their sick and afflicted and their children there were as many as 2,500 people that did bear record of Him (see 17:25). To emphasize the experience, Mormon states, "and this they did do, going forth *one by one* until they had all gone forth, and did see with their eyes and did feel with their hands" (11:15; emphasis added). The cumulative effect of the personal experience left them all worshiping Jesus and crying, "Hosanna! Blessed be the name of the Most High God!" (v. 17).

The resurrected Savior then taught that holy ordinances were to be performed individually. He detailed the procedure for performing the ordinance of baptism:

Verily I say unto you, that whoso repenteth of his sins through your words, and desireth to be baptized in my name, on this wise shall ye baptize them—Behold, ye shall go down and stand in the water, and in my name shall ye baptize them.

And now behold, these are the words which ye shall say, calling them by name, saying:

Having authority given me of Jesus Christ, I baptize you in the name of the Father, and of the Son, and of the Holy Ghost. Amen.

And then shall ye immerse them in the water, and come forth again out of the water. (3 Nephi 11:23–26)

It is significant that each person was to be specifically called by name and then immersed individually in the water by the one performing the ordinance.

Nephi baptized the disciples in the manner prescribed—one by one. The record states, "And it came to pass that Nephi went down into the water and was baptized. And he came up out of the water and began to baptize. And he baptized all those whom Jesus had chosen" (3 Nephi 19:11–12). The Book of Mormon confirms that those baptized were ministered to further:

And it came to pass when they were all baptized and had come up out of the water, the Holy Ghost did fall upon them, and they were filled with the Holy Ghost and with fire.

And behold, they were encircled about as if it were by fire; and it came down from heaven, and the multitude did witness it, and did bear record; and angels did come down out of heaven and did *minister* unto them.

And it came to pass that while the angels were *ministering* unto the disciples, behold, Jesus came and stood in the midst and *ministered* unto them. (3 Nephi 19:13–15; emphasis added)

Christ also blessed the sick among the Nephites as he had done during his mortal ministry in the Holy Land: "For I perceive that ye desire that I should show unto you what I have done unto your brethren at Jerusalem, for I see that your faith is sufficient that I should heal you" (3 Nephi 17:8). The sacred record continues, "And it came to pass that when he had thus spoken, all the multitude, with one accord, did go forth with their sick and their afflicted, and their lame, and with their blind, and with their dumb, and with all them that were afflicted in any manner; and he did heal them every one as they were brought forth unto him" (v. 9). It seems reasonable to assume that the Savior had power to heal all those present among the Nephites without their being brought forth to Him. Even before His resurrection the Savior healed people in groups without touching them and was able to heal those not within a specific proximity to Himself (see Luke 7:1–18; Mark 7:24–30). The Lord chose among the Nephites, however, to have the sick brought close to Him, and as the record implies, He touched each one personally.

Following this great healing occasion, Jesus commanded the people to bring "their little children and set them down upon the ground round about him." Then

> he took their little children, *one by one*, and blessed them, and prayed unto the Father for them.
>
> And when he had done this he wept again;
>
> And he spake unto the multitude, and said unto them: Behold your little ones.
>
> And as they looked to behold they cast their eyes towards heaven, and they saw the heavens open, and they saw angels descending out of heaven as it were in the midst of fire; and they came down and encircled those little ones about, and they were encircled about with fire; and the angels did *minister* unto them. (3 Nephi 17:11–24; emphasis added)

Mormon introduces the entire appearance narrative (see the introduction to 3 Nephi 11–26) with these words, "Jesus Christ did show himself unto the people of Nephi, as the multitude were gathered together in the land Bountiful, and did minister unto them." According to Mormon's introduction, Jesus did two things: first, He showed Himself to the people, and second,

He ministered unto them. Ministry was obviously an essential element of the visit of Christ among the Nephites.

When read together I noticed a theme about serving one by one which I had not noticed before. It became clear to me that the huge burden I felt about the issue of quality verses quantity could be solved if I put into practice the principle outlined in the scriptures above.

Immediately I began to realize that while there were times we needed to gather as a family for family prayer, family home evenings, birthdays, and other special occasions, I could spend more time with my family if I took the opportunity to do so one-on-one. Immediately, I began to see which work, school, and Church service obligations would lend themselves to bringing along a family member several times a week. I found that I could accomplish certain types of activities with them and still make it fun. In particular, business trips now became more pleasurable as one of my children or my wife accompanied me. I found myself inviting someone to go with me and at the same time promising to do something with them (stopping to get a donut or helping them get something done on the way).

I was able to accomplish my many obligations just as well as before, spending quality time—and more important—a lot more quantity time with them than I had ever before. As my children grew older this became easier and easier. They looked forward to these one-on-one experiences. They even enjoyed helping me with my work and Church service. They felt they had a stake in my life and that they were helping me, but all the while I was the real beneficiary.

My children and my spouse were more involved in my outside life than ever before. I learned something about each of them in ways that would have been impossible as we did things as a family group. I grew closer and more intimate with each of them as blocks of time, not just hours, allowed for both a quality and quantity time together.

Certainly I am not the perfect husband or father, but this one dramatic scriptural tutoring session blessed my life in ways beyond my expectation. The time together one-on-one has deepened my love and appreciation for each of my family members. My children look forward to getting away with me even for a few hours to do errands. Never again will I accept that quality can substitute for quantity any more than quantity can substitute for quality.

In the end there was harmony between what seemed to be apparent contradictions in goals and expectations because the Lord provided an answer in the scriptures for my very specific question.

CHAPTER 9

KNOWING AND LOVING JOSEPH SMITH: A PERSONAL ODYSSEY

Kenneth W. Godfrey

Latter-day Saint parents are commanded to teach their children faith in "Christ the son of the living God" (D&C 68:25) and to bring them up in "light and truth" (D&C 93:40). One of the truths children should be taught is that Joseph Smith was a prophet and that he translated the Book of Mormon by the gift and power of God. Introducing youth early to the Prophet's First Vision, and other events in his life, will set the stage for the Holy Ghost to speak peace to their minds, and they will "feel that it [the declaration that Joseph Smith is a prophet] is right" (D&C 9:8). Children armed with a testimony that Jesus is the Christ and that Joseph Smith is a true prophet of God will be able to resist temptation, overcome doubts, and resolve problems and conflicts in their families.

Kenneth W. Godfrey worked in the Church Educational system for thirty-seven years as an institute director and an area director in California, Arizona, and Utah. He has published more than 500 articles and authored or contributed to twenty-three books, including Women's Voices, *which he wrote with his wife, Audrey, and Jill Derr. His articles have appeared in the* Ensign, BYU Studies, The Illinois Historical Quarterly, Utah Historical Quarterly, Cobblestone, *and the* Journal of Mormon History. *He is the father of five children and eleven grandchildren.*

In this essay I will share experiences from my own life that will, I hope, provide examples of the importance of a testimony, will show how testimonies help us withstand temptations, even when those we admire fall, and will emphasize the value of revering the scriptures, especially those restored through Joseph Smith, the pivotal figure in the dispensation of the fulness of times. The experiences I have had teaching my own children and the youth of the Church have altered my life and changed many of their lives as well.

Sometime very early in life my father told me that during the summer of 1930, while serving as a missionary, he traveled from Montreal, Canada, to Palmyra, New York, where B. H. Roberts presided over a meeting in the Sacred Grove. Elder Roberts began the meeting by saying, "We have asked you here that this night might become a memorable occasion, memorable forever. . . . We want to know what happened here . . . and what it is beginning to mean to the whole human family."[1] Elder Roberts had written: "The groves were God's first temples, and now . . . came one [Joseph Smith] to this grove, as to a solemn temple, to submit his mind and his will to God, man's highest act of worship—self surrender."[2] Louise Lake, who also attended this meeting with B. H. Roberts recalled his powerful words and appearance that day, and wrote: "Every cell of his being was bearing witness. In the dim light, his eyes were filled with the testimony, of that spirit. I do not believe anyone could have heard B. H. Roberts as we heard him that night and doubt his knowledge. For his testimony of Christ was overwhelming."[3]

As B. H. Roberts concluded this remarkable sermon, he asked those missionaries with testimonies to stand and repeat after him, either aloud or silently, a testimony prayer bearing witness that God lives, that Jesus is the Christ, that Joseph Smith is a prophet, and that the Book of Mormon is true. Then he asked that the missionaries who had not stood, those as yet without testimonies, arise, and he prayed that the Holy Ghost would touch their hearts that they, too, might know as did he, that the gospel had been restored and that the church they belonged to was the "only true and living church upon the face of the whole earth, with which I, the Lord, am well pleased" (D&C 1:30).

My father left that magnificent meeting and tented that night with a very bright, talented musician, the son of a comparatively wealthy Holbrook, Idaho, dry farmer. Although this elder had been on his mission for almost six months, he was as yet without a testimony and had become so discouraged that evening—sensing as he did what others were experiencing yet compelled to stand with those who did not know—that he left the Sacred Grove and returned to his tent, to begin packing his gear to return home.

Dad, a seasoned missionary and full of faith, spent most of the night trying to persuade his companion to remain on his mission. He pointed out that the mission field was an ideal place to find a testimony and suggested that his companion was nearer to belief than he thought. At last Dad's words, buoyed by the brightness of a new morning, convinced his companion that he should continue his search for faith right there in Canada.

The Jonathan-and-David-like friendship forged that night between these two farm boys grew stronger as the years passed. Through the years, whenever our family visited Holbrook, Dad's companion would recount this story and tell us how thankful he was that our father had persuaded him to remain in Canada, because he, just as Dad said he would, found a firm testimony there.

Hearing and re-hearing this Sacred Grove experience, as shared by two men I loved and admired, greatly influenced my life. Learning early that a testimony mattered, I often asked God to give me one. Sometimes while singing "Oh, how lovely was the morning!" I believed I could actually hear the bees hum, and the birds sing, and the "music ringing thru the grove." Every now and then a chill caressed my back as I sang the words, "For he saw the living God." While I did not always recognize those chills as the beginnings of a testimony that they were, I began very early a love affair with the plow-boy prophet, Joseph Smith.

Dad, Mother, and speakers in Church meetings, especially those of the two-and-one-half-minute-talk kind, often told the story of Joseph Smith suffering from typhoid fever and osteomyelitis when just seven years old. These sermons and sermonettes emphasized his refusal of liquor proffered to lessen the pain. I was moved by his courage and his wish to have his father hold him instead of being bound, and by his desire that his mother not be permitted to witness his suffering. The months of painful limping, too, I never forgot. Only after becoming an adult did I learn that the surgery on his leg was one of the first of many miracles in his life. Had the Smiths not been living near Dartmouth College where Dr. Nathan Smith taught, it is likely that Joseph's leg would have been amputated. God, it appears, wanted a two-legged prophet to head the last dispensation of the fulness of times.

Sitting in the mission home early in November 1953, I listened as Lynn McKinley told the more than two hundred departing missionaries that we would be useless servants and unable to withstand the rigors of missionary life unless we knew that Joseph had seen God and Christ and that the Book of Mormon had been translated by the gift and power of God through the Urim and Thummim.

I believed but did not *know*. So while Brother McKinley continued his sermon I prayed, believing God could inspire the speaker and answer my prayer simultaneously. Suddenly, without warning, an indescribable assurance, companioned by a slight shiver, came over all that was I, and somehow all I was knew absolutely that Joseph Smith was a prophet and that the Book of Mormon was true. I had read the Book of Mormon only once, yet I knew that Nephi, Jacob, Enos, the Almas, the Moronis, and Mormon were real people who once lived somewhere on the American continent. Startled that my prayer had been answered so quickly, I hardly heard anything else Brother McKinley said as I basked in the thrill of my new knowledge. No longer did I merely believe; I knew!

A few days later, after a train ride across the United States, I arrived with three other missionaries in Atlanta, Georgia, head-quarters of the Southern States Mission. After a weekend of ori-entation, I was sent on to Florida where I met my companion for the first time. He was a strong, sturdy, ex-Marine who had fought in Korea and still had nightmares over some of his expe-riences there. Not active in the Church during most of his youth, he had undergone a life-changing experience when his sergeant, who had become a father figure, died in his arms near Seoul, Korea. With his discharge came a mission call. And now here I was, the first new missionary he had been asked to train.

As we briskly walked, Marine-like, to the tracting area, he informed me that it was customary for a new missionary to take the first door on his initial day in the mission field. The mission home experience and the prayers of my parents so motivated and inspired me that I believed that, as with God, nothing was impossible.

As I knocked on my first door only a screen door separated me from those in the house. Standing in the kitchen doorway I could barely see the outline of a large man who shouted, "You're the Mormon missionaries, come on in!" Wow, I thought, mis-sionary work is just as easy as those mission home folk said it would be. Seated in the living room, my companion quietly informed me that it was also a mission tradition that newly arrived elders teach the first discussion in the first home. "No problem," I said.

I had uttered only a sentence or two, however, when the burly man called a halt and declared he wanted to ask me a ques-tion or two about the translation of the Book of Mormon. Secure in the knowledge that my companion could answer any question, I nodded, and the questions—more like statements of fact—poured forth: "Why did Joseph Smith take a rock, place it in an old black hat, pull the hat over his eyes, and pretend he was translating plates made of gold? Did you know that Martin Har-ris, one of the three witnesses, declared that Joseph Smith was often drunk as he translated the record? Did you know that David Whitmer, another witness, wrote that Joseph Smith did not need to have the plates present to translate? Finally, how do you explain the thousands and thousands of changes that have seriously altered the text of the Book of Mormon so that the present edition is much different than the first edition published by E. B. Grandin?"

Surprised that he seemed to know so much about early Church history, I confidently turned to my companion, inviting his knowledge and forensic skills. I was completely surprised, then, when my companion told the man that he had not been a regular church-goer as a youth and had little knowledge of the Church's history and its scriptures. "Elder Godfrey, on the other hand," he continued, "has always been active in the Church, received individual awards each year, as well as perfect atten-dance certificates some years, so he will answer your questions," and he sat back in his chair. For the third or fourth time in my life I knew real fear. None of my Sunday School or seminary teachers had prepared me to answer the man's queries (at least not when I was listening), yet I felt some obligation to respond in a way that would save the Prophet Joseph Smith's honor.

Feeling precious little confidence I heard myself say, "I do not know the answer to the questions you asked, although I am confident that there are satisfactory answers. What I do know is that the Holy Ghost told me only a few days ago that Joseph Smith is a prophet and the Book of Mormon, however it was translated, is a true record of a people who lived somewhere on the American continent. Furthermore, I know that the Holy Ghost, who told me these things, does not lie."[4]

Looking back on that initial missionary experience I am more convinced now than I was then that my answer was not a bad one. Still, I resolved that day to learn everything I could about Joseph Smith and the history of the Church. I believe, too, that God knew what my first missionary encounter would be and quickly gave me a testimony so that my faith and Joseph Smith's honor would remain sure when confronted by a hostile questioner. God, I believe, would not have given me such assurance had I known nothing about Joseph Smith and the Book of Mormon. All those meetings I attended as a youth, those frequent readings of the Joseph Smith History and the Book of Mormon were not entirely wasted because I had absorbed more than I knew.

Taking our children to Church with us, and reading the scriptures together as a family, as well as teaching by example the importance of personal scripture study, will enable our own families to absorb the gospel. The beginnings of faith are often found in Joseph Smith's history and in the beginning chapters of the Book of Mormon.

While still a teenager I learned that somehow faith, testimony, and conduct are linked. When I was just fourteen years of age the baseball team sponsored by the small community in which I resided won the championship, beating a fine team from a much larger town in the valley. We won the game by a score of 2-1 in one of the most exciting contests I had ever witnessed. As I made my way to our family car for the five-mile journey home, I passed the billiard parlor and saw many of my heroes, the town's sluggers, drinking beer. Even two members of the bishopric were imbibing. A few hours later, deeply troubled, I sat on a one-legged stool and milked one of our cows near my father, who was only two cows away. I told him what I had seen and expressed my disappointment in witnessing active Church members and good men drinking. (That some members of the team were drinking did not surprise nor trouble me.) Dad asked me if I knew anyone who would not drink, regardless of the social pressure. My Sunday School teacher, a former bishop, stake president's counselor, and exile from Mexico, was the second person whose name came to my mind. The first was my father. "You would not, nor would Brother Naegle," I answered.

"Why do you say that?" Dad asked.

"Because you both have real testimonies," I answered.

Even as a boy I knew that true faith and an actual testimony changed behavior and would make no allowance for beer consumption, regardless of the occasion. I was also conscious that repentance is possible and that while the Spirit is willing the flesh is sometimes weak.

Not many months passed before my belief was tested. As my friends and I celebrated the Twenty-Fourth of July in a nearby community, we met and began conversing with some young ladies. As I spoke with the girls my friends drifted off, and upon returning to the car I discovered they had somehow purchased a case of beer and had already started drinking. Everyone, except me, drank some beer as we drove to another larger town. I was cajoled, teased, and threatened that I too should imbibe. Suddenly the driver, who had also been drinking, stopped the automobile, whereupon my buddies told me that if I did not consume at least part of a bottle of beer I would be thrown to the ground and forced to drink. Using humor, I finally persuaded the group that they needed someone sober to drive the car. Somehow what I said finally made sense and, beerless, I got behind the wheel, the crisis over.

My determination not to consume alcohol on that Pioneer Day was not a spur-of-the-moment decision. Dad, several years prior to my Twenty-Fourth of July confrontation with my beer-drinking friends, became aware that God often made covenants with his children. These covenants are clearly explained in the scriptures. Therefore, my father concluded that his own children might be able to ward off temptations if they were obligated by covenant with him. One evening, as we milked cows together, I made a covenant with Dad that we would never smoke or drink tea, coffee, or alcohol unless we did it together. (Strange as it seems, when I was with Dad I was somehow never tempted to smoke or drink.) Through my friends' taunts and threats that night it seemed I could still hear the milk hitting the bottom of the pail reminding me of the covenant I had made with Dad. Testimony and covenants, I learned, do alter behavior, even in the face of overwhelming social pressure.

Later, as I raised my own children, I sometimes called their attention to covenants they had made. When we lived in Arizona, my son David played on a little league football team. The final play-off game was scheduled the same time as Primary. David's mother was the Primary president and very much wanted, as did I, our children to be good examples. David did not want to let his teammates down nor did he want to offend his Heavenly Father; he was caught in a dilemma. As we talked together, I asked him if he remembered the covenant he had made at baptism, calling his attention to Mosiah 18:8–9, and said that he had told his Heavenly Father that he would stand as a witness of God at all times and in all things and would serve Him and keep His commandments. Then I told him that Heavenly Father also gave us agency and left us free to choose, and that if he would make the game and Primary a matter of prayer his mother and I would honor his decision. The following morning David appeared in our bedroom well before the sun and declared he would read the scriptures for thirty minutes before the game and for thirty minutes after, but he would play football.

A decade passed and our family lived in Pittsburgh, Pennsylvania, where I was mission president. We resided there when the Steelers were winning Super Bowls and Three Rivers Stadium was always sold out. David, a senior in high school now and first assistant in the priest quorum in our ward, was also in the high school marching band. The band was invited to march at halftime at a Steelers game. The contest, however, was to be played on Sunday.

Sunday evening as I returned home from a long day of taking care of mission business, my wife told me that I should go to David's room and tell him how proud I was of him because he had not marched with the band, had taken a ten percent reduction in his grade for not participating, and instead had attended all his Church meetings and performed his priest quorum duties. I walked into his upstairs room and found him reading (more likely *Sports Illustrated* than the scriptures) and began to express my appreciation to him for the decision he had made. Suddenly he smiled and said, "Oh, Dad it was no biggie. Don't you remember the covenant I made at baptism?" When decisions began to really count in his life he had remembered!

In graduate school I became a serious student of LDS history.

I tried then, and I still try, to read everything written by or about Joseph Smith. I have pondered and taught the different accounts of the First Vision and each one has increased my faith. Arthur Henry King has written:

> When I was first brought to read Joseph Smith's story, I was deeply impressed. I wasn't inclined to be impressed. As a stylistician I have spent my life being disinclined to be impressed. So when I read his story, I thought to myself, this is an extraordinary thing. This is an astonishingly matter-of-fact and cool account. This man is not trying to persuade me of anything. . . . He is not trying to make me cry or feel ecstatic. . . . I could see that this man was telling the truth.[5]

Joseph Smith's account carries with it a spiritual power, a simplicity, an elucidation of the facts that convinces readers that the events he describes took place.

While serving as a mission president in Pennsylvania I was asked to speak at the Pittsburgh Theological Seminary. I took my assistants with me. As I addressed those men who were about to become ministers in a variety of Protestant churches, the impression came to me that they believed the only reason I was a Mormon was because I had been born and raised in my church. When I told them my impression, several smiled and nodded their heads. I said, "That is not the reason I am a Latter-day Saint, but instead of my telling you the real reason I am a Mormon, I am going to ask my assistant, Elder Zeller, to tell you why he joined the Church. He is the only member of his family that belongs to the LDS Church and he joined when he was about seventeen or eighteen years old. Furthermore, he is bright enough to be accepted at any university in the country, including Harvard, Yale, Princeton, Brown, or even the University of Pittsburgh."

Elder Zeller almost fell off his chair, having had no warning that he would address that group. But, being obedient, he did as I asked. After relating a few things about his life and his search for the true church, he began to recite Joseph Smith's account of his First Vision, word for word, as he had memorized it. He came to the words, "I saw two Personages, whose brightness and glory defy all description, standing above me in the air. One of them spake unto me, calling me by name and said, pointing to the other—This is My Beloved Son. Hear Him!" (JS-H, 1:17). The spirit of the Lord filled the room, bearing witness that Elder Zeller spoke the truth. Some eyes began to tear. Then Elder Zeller said, "That is why I joined the Church, because God the Father and Jesus Christ appeared to Joseph Smith and later through him restored the true church to the earth."

After Elder Zeller concluded his testimony I said, "That is why I am a Mormon, too. It makes little difference that my great-great-grandfather was converted as a grown man, that my great-grandfather was a Mormon, my grandfather and my father, too. I am a Latter-day Saint because, like Elder Zeller, I know that Joseph Smith was a prophet." Like Joseph Smith and Elder Zeller, I also spoke truth.

Each time I teach, study, and ponder the Joseph Smith history, I feel like Oliver Cowdery when he wrote while translating for Joseph Smith, "These were days never to be forgotten—to sit under the sound of a voice dictated by the inspiration of heaven." (JS-H, 58n). I believe that reading Joseph Smith's history is as close as we can come to sitting under the sound of a voice dictated by the inspiration of heaven.

While walking alone along the streets and lanes of Nauvoo, where I lived for a time, I sometimes thought I could hear Joseph's voice, speaking words such as "Let thy bowels also be full of charity towards all men . . . let virtue garnish thy thoughts unceasingly" (D&C 121:45). "Whatever principle of intelligence we attain unto in this life, it will rise with us in the resurrection" (D&C 130:18). "The glory of God is intelligence" (D&C 93:36). Or "No power or influence can or ought to be maintained by virtue of the priesthood, only by persuasion, by long-suffering, by gentleness and meekness, and by love unfeigned" (D&C 121:41). A friend and colleague of mine calls such pithy statements "zingers": they are beautifully crafted, exude truth and speak to the heart. Joseph could not have composed such phrases on his own, he had to be inspired. The scriptures, which come from God, and went through Joseph's mind and were subsequently written down, contain hundreds of "zingers" that, if lived will, with the assistance of Christ, help save us.

For more than thirty years I taught in various institutes of the Church a course titled "Joseph Smith's Life and Thought." At the conclusion of each course the students were asked to write down some of their feelings about the Prophet. One girl declared that when she first came to class she did not like Joseph Smith, but after only ten weeks of being with him, she now both loved him and revered him as God's prophet. An older man stated that he often felt hopeless as it seemed certain he could never grow into celestial material, but after learning about Joseph's faith in people and the courage with which he overcame the obstacles in his life, he now experienced a surge of hope. A girl wrote that because of what she had learned about Joseph in the class she had decided "to stay with the Church." The Prophet's life, in all its complexity, has at its core faith, goodness, conviction, and sacrifice, and these same attributes are contagious.

A number of years ago, in the company of three or four historians, I visited the Independence, Missouri, home of Lynn Smith, Joseph Smith's great-great-grandson. We were shown some of Joseph Smith's schoolbooks, the wedding ring he gave Emma, his hairbrush, comb, razor, a chest of drawers that belonged to Joseph and Emma, and other memorabilia. We held these objects that had been Joseph's and talked about this man whom author Donna Hill called "The First Mormon." Then we gathered around a grand piano and sang "The Spirit of God Like a Fire Is Burning," after which our host led us as we knelt in prayer. While the prayer was being offered, the Holy Ghost spoke to my mind and my heart and reminded me that Joseph was God's prophet. Surprised by the joy I experienced, I thanked God that night as I knelt beside my motel bed that I knew

Joseph and knew he was His prophet. Daryl Chase wrote a book titled *Joseph Smith As He Lives in the Hearts of His People,* and Chase was right, Joseph lives, his message is relevant, and the faith and hope he restored to people seeking the way home continues to brighten our existence.

Once I interviewed Hugh Nibley about his memories of his grandfather Charles W. Nibley, who served as the Church's Presiding Bishop and also as a counselor in the First Presidency. At one point during the interview I asked Brother Nibley if he had anything that belonged to his grandfather. "Yes," he said. "I have a copy of the first edition of the Book of Mormon published in England in 1840. It was given to Grandfather by Brigham Young and it has a note from Brother Brigham on the first page." He got up and retrieved the book. After I had looked at it and the inscription, Nibley sat down once more in his chair, still holding the Book of Mormon. It fell open and he declared, "My gosh, this passage is describing the Urim and Thummim and using words the ancients would have used." Remarkably the plowboy prophet had struck again; he got things just right. Brother Nibley is a brilliant scholar who has given his whole academic life to a study of the Book of Mormon and Joseph Smith. This familiarity has engendered an impressive and life-changing reverence for the restored gospel.

I have learned, along with many others, the importance of sharing with our children when they are very young the Joseph Smith story and its importance in gaining a personal testimony. Reading the Prophet's account of seeing God in Palmyra in the spring of 1820, and the coming forth of the Book of Mormon are often precursors for obtaining a testimony that Joseph was God's prophet and that the Book of Mormon is true. A testimony of these truths alters our lives and our conduct. Making covenants with our children and explaining carefully how the covenants they will make at baptism may be renewed in partaking of the sacrament plays an important role in keeping them on the path that leads home.

Finally, Joseph Smith taught us to teach one another words

of wisdom: "Yea, seek ye out of the best books words of wisdom; seek learning, even by study and also by faith" (D&C 88:118).

Long ago I discussed these words with my Doctrine and Covenants students in an 8:30 A.M. class. After we had listed the best books they had read, I asked the class what the very best books really were and they responded, "the scriptures." Then I pulled a first edition of the Book of Mormon from behind the podium where I had concealed it. "This is a first edition of the Book of Mormon," I said.

We heard a gasp, and a young man from Korea said, "Is that really a first edition?"

"Yes," I replied.

"I don't think anyone in my country has ever seen one of those," he declared. "Could I touch it?"

"Of course," I replied.

He made his way to where I stood, tears dripping off his chin. He took the book, caressed its pages, and quietly said, "When I return home, I will tell my people that I held and turned the pages of a first edition of the Book of Mormon; they will be very pleased." Then he clasped the book and held it near his heart, all the while shedding tears of joy. The class, including the teacher, left the room that day, having had a spiritual experience that improved our faith and our appreciation for the Book of Mormon. Our children can develop that same kind of love, too, for the book and for Joseph Smith, the book's translator.

"Scriptural memories, spiritual memories," Neal A. Maxwell tells us, "can be lost in a generation."[6] Years ago my cousin won a scholarship and was accepted as a doctoral student at a large, prestigious midwestern university. He and his wife loaded all they had into their automobile and a small trailer and spent their last night in Utah at the home of his parents, my uncle and aunt. Early the next morning, well before it was light, he and his wife appeared in his parents' bedroom. "Dad," he said, arousing his father from a deep sleep. "Do you remember on Saturday mornings when my sisters and I were small that we used to get in bed with you and Mom and you would tell us stories?"

"Yes son, I remember," his father answered.

"Well," Allen (not his real name) continued, "could Mary (not her real name) and I get in bed with you and Mom?"

"Aren't you a little old for that?" my uncle queried.

"Yes," Allen declared, "but I would like to hear those old stories again. You see I'm scared about going east, frightened of graduate school, and I think those stories will help us."

So my cousin and his wife got into bed, and his mom and dad told old stories for an hour or more. Then Allen spoke, "Thanks Dad and Mom, I think we can face graduate school now." Dressed and full of his mom's breakfast, Allen and Mary headed east with those enduring old stories of faith, sacrifice, and consecration fresh in their minds, retracing in reverse the trail his great-grandmother walked when only six years old.

The scriptures and those old stories of Joseph Smith and the Mormon pioneers in every land are like my uncle's tales. Not only are they true, but they help us remember who we are, from whence we came, and how to return safely home. My knowing and loving Joseph Smith for more than six decades now has made me, I hope, a better traveler, and a better parent as I journey home.

NOTES

1. Truman G. Madsen, *Defender of the Faith, The B. H. Roberts Story* (Salt Lake City: Bookcraft, 1980), p. 368.

2. Ibid.

3. Ibid.

4. This is the way I remember my experience of many years ago. I would not be willing to be burned at the stake if this representation is not one hundred percent accurate.

5. Arthur Henry King, *The Abundance of the Heart* (Salt Lake City City: Bookcraft, 1986), pp. 200–201.

6 Neal A. Maxwell, "The Pathway of Discipleship," *Ensign*, September 1998, p. 10.

CHAPTER 10

HIS EYES WILL BE HEALED: ALMA 34 AND A CHILD'S PRAYER

Jane D. Brady

I could tell that Sam was paying attention. We were reading Alma, chapter 34 while sitting around the kitchen table. Sure, he listened intently to the Book of Mormon battle scenes and he seemed to pay attention better when we had him read every tenth verse or so, but kids' minds do wander. Still, I remember distinctly the feeling I had as we read—a "he's listening" impression.

We had made a goal to finish reading the Book of Mormon before Sam's baptism in the summer of 1998. To help the kids (and us) stay motivated we got one of those charts that says "I Have Read the Book of Mormon" with several squares in each letter of the saying to signify each individual chapter. The kids were excited to mark off each square. Thanks to that, and to our sly idea of feeding them some kind of little treat right before bed, they would sit quietly at the kitchen table and listen while they munched. At least they were quiet and they sat still. Who could say if they were really listening, really hearing?

Jane D. Brady lives in an old stone house with her husband, Ken, children Sam, McKenna, and Emma Jane, and cat Oreo. She alternates teaching Gospel Doctrine with Elder C. Max Caldwell in their American Fork, Utah, ward. She has a master's in English from Brigham Young University and is the editor of Mourning Those Who Mourn *with Steven Walker.*

The goal was a good one, we knew that. Certainly nothing *bad* could come from following a commandment, from inviting the Spirit into our home every day. But when children are young, it is difficult to determine what kind of effect the scriptures are having on them. It felt more like we *weren't doing something wrong* than it felt like we were doing something right, if you know what I mean.

Let me remind you of some of the words comprising Alma 34:

> Therefore may God grant unto you, my brethren, that ye may begin to exercise your faith unto repentance, that ye begin to call upon his holy name, that he would have mercy upon you;
> Yea, cry unto him for mercy; for he is mighty to save.
> Yea, humble yourselves, and continue in prayer unto him.
> Cry unto him when ye are in your fields, yea, over all your flocks.
> Cry unto him in your houses, yea, over all your household, both morning, mid-day, and evening.

"Why are they crying?" McKenna asked.

"They're not," Sam answered. "He's talking about praying. He's saying when you should pray."

"When *should* you pray?" she asked. (Yep, she's four.)

"Everywhere!" Sam said, a little impatient at this point.

> Cry unto him over the crops of your fields, that ye may prosper in them.
> Cry over the flocks of your fields, that they may increase.
> But this is not all; ye must pour out your souls in your closets, and your secret places, and in your wilderness.
> Yea, and when you do not cry unto the Lord, let your hearts be full, drawn out in prayer unto him continually for your welfare, and also for the welfare of those who are around you.

"Could I pray for a Nintendo 64?" Sam wanted to know.

"What do you think?" Ken responded. (You can tell he's had experience with these kinds of questions.)

"Why not? He says to pray about the flocks, about things they want. I want an N-64."

"Prayer *is* about things that you want, but things that you want which are good. Things that God wants you to have and knows are best for you," Ken responded.

"I don't see what's wrong with wanting an N-64. I don't see how that wouldn't be best for me."

"That's the point, though; we *don't* always see what's best for us, but God always does. He always knows."

Yet Sam had a good point. Weren't there things that *I* wanted enough to hope for, even pray and plead for, not caring what was best for me, just focusing on my deeply felt need? I thought about that as Ken read the rest of the chapter. Then, in verse 38 my answer seemed to come:

> That ye contend no more against the Holy Ghost, but that ye receive it, and take upon you the name of Christ; that ye humble yourselves even to the dust, and worship God, in whatsoever place ye may be in, in spirit and in truth; and that ye live in thanksgiving daily, for the many mercies and blessings which he doth bestow upon you.

It was months later before I remembered that particular evening around the dinner table, our discussion of Alma 34, and the distinct feeling I'd had that Sam had been listening.

> Prayer is the act by which the will of the Father and the will of the child are brought into correspondence with each other. (Bible Dictionary, "Prayer")

Sam had a problem. He'd been playing a game on the computer and his eyes were beginning to hurt. He so wanted to keep playing that he kept going until the pain became unbearable. At that point he panicked. In his seven-year-old mind he imagined the worst. Would the pain ever stop? Was he going blind? Sam decided this emergency was exactly the kind of thing he should pray about. Alone in the study he folded his arms and prayed for the pain to stop. He believed in God. He knew God was powerful. He knew that God could stop the pain; he had faith in that. So he prayed and prayed, and then he said amen.

Nothing changed.

He waited for a few minutes (a long time for him) and still nothing happened. If anything, the pain was getting worse. He squeezed his eyes as tightly as he could but he couldn't shut out the pain.

> The object of prayer is not to change the will of God, but to secure for ourselves and for others blessings that God is already willing to grant, but that are made conditional on our asking for them. (Bible Dictionary, "Prayer")

So far Sam's story wasn't too surprising to me. I know the goodness in Sam's soul. I know he tries to do what is right. What surprised me was what came next: a giant leap of faith, so big that many adults never take it. Sam realized that his prayer had been wrong. He had been *telling* God what to do instead of *asking* Him what to do. He started over. This time he explained his problem to God and then told Him he would do whatever He said. He wanted the pain to stop and would do whatever it took, even if it meant to stop playing his game—something he really didn't want to do. Even if it meant coming to tell me, which surely meant no more computer games. Sam remembers saying amen and sitting there for a moment with his arms folded, just sitting quietly and waiting. Then came, strongly, into his heart, the message, "Tell your mom. She'll know what to do."

> Blessings require work or effort on our part before we can obtain them. (Bible Dictionary, "Prayer")

When Sam came to me I knew immediately that his problem

was serious. He was choked up, he even had a difficult time getting the words out. Finally he communicated to me that his eyes hurt and that he was very worried about them. Knowing how seldom Sam complains, I figured they really were stinging. I knew he had been reading all morning and since then had been playing on the computer, so I assumed his eyes were just tired, aching from overuse. At first I thought I'd tell him to rest them for a while, that he should just lie down with his eyes closed and I would put a cool, moist cloth over them. But as soon as I thought that, I knew it wasn't right. I knew Sam needed me. I decided to drop off the little girls at a friend's house to play, and then Sam and I went alone to the doctor's office. Although I wasn't as worried as Sam, I wanted to take him seriously. I wanted to take care of him completely.

> Prayer is a form of work, and is an appointed means for obtaining the highest of all blessings. (Bible Dictionary, "Prayer")

Though the doctor was busy, the nurse saw us immediately. She could tell, as I could, that Sam was upset, deeply concerned. She was very gentle and attentive to him. She looked carefully into his eyes. She had him read the eye chart. Then she asked him questions about what he had been doing all day. Coming to the same conclusion that I had, she told him it was important to do all kinds of different things with his eyes—from big things like catching a ball to small things like reading a book. Now that his eyes were overtired from too much strain he'd need to rest them for a long while. She gave him some drops to help him to feel better. And Sam really did feel better. He knew he wasn't going to go blind or die. He knew that I loved him. He knew that God had heard him.

On the way home Sam explained to me all that had happened. He told me about his two prayers and the big change in between. He said he knew he was going to be all right now.

> There are many instances of Jesus healing the blind. Indeed,

part of his mission as foretold by Isaiah included "recovering of sight to the blind." . . . In addition to the healing of physical blindness, the mission of Jesus included curing blindness to the things of the spirit. He made an application of this in John 9:5 when, in conjunction with healing the man born blind, he declared that he (Jesus) was "the light of the world." (Bible Dictionary, "Blindness")

The Light of Christ will lead the honest soul who "hearkeneth to the voice" to find the tru[th]. (Bible Dictionary, "Light of Christ")

I imagine Sam, eighteen years old, with some problem, some difficulty that seems as if it will never go away. I can believe that he would pray about it. We've prayed with him since the day he was born. We've brought him to Church. We've tried to teach him the right things. And who doesn't pray in a crisis? Who doesn't plead with God to make it all go away? What I hope with all of my heart is that Sam will remember the scriptures that we've read with him and remember the examples of the prophets. I hope he will pray, not for his own will but for God's will to be done. Because if he does, his eyes will be healed, and one day they will open upon the face of God.

CHAPTER 11

EXPERIMENT ON HIS WORD: THE VALUE IN TRAINING UP A CHILD

Elaine A. Cannon

The genesis of my life with the scriptures, the basic thread of it—or better, the iron rod of it—was in my grasp from my earliest remembrance. I have a recurring mental image of sitting on my mother's lap sipping from the common sacrament cup passed to my mother by a beloved old ward member whose face was heavy with hair on both sides of his mouth. Mother then turned the cup around from the place where his sipping lips had been and, with the soft side of her wrist, she wiped a spot for me to take the sacrament water.

And I did drink, cautioned by Mother's whisper in my ear, "Now this is so you will remember Jesus."

Jesus had a beard, too. I knew that from the picture of Him at home. Much later I learned about His bitter cup.

In the days of the common cup, the newly organized Capitol Hill Ward met in the spruced up stable house of the McCune

Elaine A. Cannon is a former general president of the Young Women organization of The Church of Jesus Christ of Latter-day Saints. She has also served as associate editor of Church magazines for youth and their leaders. She is the award-winning author of many books, including, most recently, The Christmas Crèche, Mary's Child, *and* Minerva! The Story of an Artist with a Mission. *She and her family reside in Salt Lake City, Utah.*

mansion a block or two south of the Utah State Capitol in Salt Lake City, Utah. My father served as the member of the bishopric in charge of the building committee for a new chapel west of the State Capitol. When that stone church was completed, Daddy saw to it that the common chalice was replaced with individual cups of pure ivory.

Half a century later I was presented with one of those pure ivory sacrament cups. It had been discovered in the attic of the Capitol Hill ward building during renovation. I treasure that elegant little cup and try to resist being a bore by showing it off. I would love somehow to have the sacrament passed to me again in that cup. Many years before that presentation to me, my older brother Aldon Junior was ordained a priest. He had just turned seventeen and was first assigned to officiate at the sacrament table using those very ivory cups for the service.

In our family, that was an Occasion. Mother was a student of elocution and would not permit Junior to give a skimpy recitation with mumbling tongue. The family scriptures were laid open (people did not have personal scripture sets in those days) to the passages containing the sacramental prayers (see D&C 20:77–79). The solemn training began. Part of the practice was an explanation of the phrases so that when Junior uttered the special prayer, the audience would grasp its meaning.

That explanation in itself was life-changing for me. For example, I heard within me a new idea at the words: "That they are willing to take upon them the name of thy Son." I had my daddy's last name already—Anderson—and in his house I did certain things that he required of me as his daughter. Now I was to take upon me the name of Heavenly Father's Son! I was not yet twelve years old but I felt the press of personal responsibility. There were things I had to do in that regard.

As my brother practiced the prayers, I hung around drinking them in. Then, that Sunday at sacrament meeting, I listened carefully to see if Junior performed his duty as rehearsed. I judged him perfect and was not surprised that he grew up to become a federal judge.

Having been reared in an environment attentive to the spirit behind the letter of the law and ritual, as well as having been taught to rise to the Lord's occasion, the tradition of seeking guidance from the word of God has been carried forth into succeeding generations. Wo! Wo! Wo be unto the errant descendant who dared slur over the sacramental prayer or who failed to use the correct language of prayer whenever addressing Heavenly Father. You see, just as we learn French or German at school, we learned a second language from our parents and the scriptures— the language of God. *Thee, thou, thy, thine, wouldst, wilt,* and so on became familiar to us in our prayers at home. This eliminated self-consciousness about using this language out loud before a congregation or in a sacred circle of prayer such as when a baby is blessed, a member is confirmed or given a healing blessing, or if a guest is kneeling with us around the dining room table.

All the days of my life, I have found joy in a prayer given by one literate in the language and spirit of God. During my term as a General President of the Young Women organization for The Church of Jesus Christ of Latter-day Saints, we held several enlightening sessions on the language of prayer and the proper usage of titles of deity. This was done so that the women called to serve on the governing board filling assignments to edify youth leaders around the world would pray and refer to deity with traditional respect. Our philosophy was that if the sisters were familiar with the language and order of prayer they could instruct their families. General Authorities of the Church were our professors in this pursuit. Janet Palmer of the Young Women Board, who at the time was head of the department of English at Westminster College in Salt Lake City, helped us with usage. I believe the scripture that suggests that we do not have to be commanded in all things (see D&C 58:26). No one insisted that we were to engage in such activity, but we were glad we did, for it was insightful.

Success in strengthening oneself, guiding an adult, or rearing a child for a life of religious contribution or for self-discipline hangs on this hook: "Train up a child in the way he should go:

and when he is old, he will not depart from it" (Proverbs 22:6).

It is understandable that Nephi mourned over those who had not been taught to believe. Even when the word was given to them in simplicity and plainness, because of their wickedness, they did not receive it. Some because of their stiffneckedness would not search for knowledge and this closed the door to yet "greater knowledge."

Nephi said: "For if ye would hearken unto the Spirit which teacheth a man to pray ye would know that ye must pray; for the evil spirit teacheth not a man to pray, he teacheth him that he must not pray" (2 Nephi 32:8).

A specific experience confirmed for me the value in training up a child so that when he is grown he will know the path to follow. Some years ago during a jaunt to St. George the jam-packed car necessitated a few ground rules for our traveling group. Although we were all related, our ages differed greatly, and each came from a separate home. Since we would share a motel room, Great-grandmother would have a bed to herself; I, the grandmother, would share a bed with my career-girl daughter; the two scampy preschool boy cousins (my grandsons) would bed down in sleeping bags in front of the big television set.

When we arrived at our room, I suggested a kneeling prayer around Great-grandmother's bed to dedicate our temporary home-away-from-home. Each time my own family had moved over the years we had held a dedicatory prayer in the new home, that it might be blessed with God's protection and sweet spirit. I must admit that in this case, I was also thinking about prayer as a way to forestall those two destroying angels from turning the place into a disaster area. It also seemed a golden moment to teach my grandsons.

We knelt around the bed, and I was voice. Just as I closed the prayer, three-year-old Jake said, "Wait! Don't anybody stand up. Now I want each one to pray and I will be last." (Had he been taught about priesthood leadership or what?)

That little child did lead, and we all learned sweet things from each prayer. When he then insisted on reading the scriptures together out loud, I realized that my daughter deserved credit for training him well in a valued tradition. He was even sure there was a Holy Bible in the motel room. Now a young man, Jake still prays and reads the scriptures, but in Spanish, as a returned Guatemalan missionary.

The benefits of training up a child to live by the word of God are numerous, varied, beneficial, and beautiful. My husband, Jim, and I learned this at the beginning of our parenting years. We had four children under age five, and then, before we could catch our breath, we had six children under age eleven, whether we needed them or not! By then Jim had been called to be bishop for a third time. He had started a printing and publishing business with a weekly newspaper which meant two all-night sessions each week away from home in addition to his assignments as bishop. Our high ideals for a civilized lifestyle often escaped us altogether, so Sundays offered precious time together.

Before we were married, Jim and I had individually become interested in the question of why the Lamanites differed from the Nephites when they both stemmed from Father Lehi and Sariah. It seemed a telling alert to any parents that moral agency could be wrongly used. The explanation for me began with King Benjamin, who told his people that it was not possible for Father Lehi to remember all that his children needed to know when they left Jerusalem for the wilderness. However, with the help of the plates of Laban and the plates of Nephi, the posterity of Father Lehi learned to read and understand God's mysteries, and thus they had God's commandments always before their eyes. King Benjamin said: "Were it not for these things, which have been kept and preserved by the hand of God, . . . we should have been like unto our brethren, the Lamanites, who know nothing concerning these things" (Mosiah 1:5).

Made sense to me. Learning the truth is important for any generation, given the reality of an active adversary who has been conniving for the souls of men since the war in heaven.

Jim, on the other hand, was a fan of the terse scribes

included in the unique book of Omni, which spans a period of about 150 years. They didn't record much, but the value in training up a child is evident. Omni admitted to being a wicked man, but was converted to the importance of keeping records for the next generation. Amaleki was the son of Abinadom, who was the son of Chemish, who was the brother of Amaron, who was the son of Omni, who was the son of Jarom—and each in turn made a brief but telling record of how people get off track. Amaleki wrote of the condition of the people of Zarahemla when Mosiah discovered them. Because they had no scriptures, they were a warring people, in confusion. Their language had become corrupted, they did not believe in the Creator or know anything about his principles to help mankind live successfully and peace-fully.

These parents had not taught their children.

But Adam and Eve "made all things known unto their sons and their daughters" (Moses 5:12). So did Father Lehi. King Benjamin was diligent in this, and all the prophets in our day have so counseled. Joseph Smith said, "I teach them correct principles and they govern themselves."[1] It remains for parents in our day to follow their inspired leaders, especially to see to it that correct principles are taught so that their children have enough knowledge to govern their own decisions.

These are the flat facts behind why Jim and I started a Sunday scripture read-aloud even though the children were barely able to read. We knew that our posterity should experience the sweet and saving truths of the gospel for themselves by searching the word with their own senses—seeing, hearing, speaking the word out loud. We made some personal sacrifice in groceries so that each one had a set of scriptures, except the toddler, who had a Golden Book of Jesus from which he took a turn "reading."

It was perhaps the best gift we gave our children through all the years.

Jim introduced us to this tradition by telling us a tender story from his Hawaiian mission days. A worn Bible was his visual aid. In a country town on the island of Maui, a young boy lay close to death with a dangerously high fever. The doctor had done everything he knew. There were no life-saving miracle antibiotics at that time. The elders had been called in to administer a healing blessing. Jim explained to our family, "Before the anointing, I asked the boy if he knew about Jesus. He nodded his head weakly without opening his eyes. Then I put this Bible on his chest and laid his hand on it so he could feel it. I told him this was the sacred book that described all about Jesus and the good things He did—how He placed His hands on sick people and made them well. I read out loud from Mark 9 (we all opened our Bibles to Mark 9) where it is recorded that a father brought his son to Jesus to be healed from a terrible illness. The scripture says: 'Jesus said unto him, If thou canst believe, all things are possible to him that believeth. And straightway the father of the child cried out, and said with tears, Lord, I believe; help thou my unbelief' (Mark 9:23–24).

"I wasn't certain that this sick boy was well enough or trained sufficiently to understand what I was saying," Jim related, "but we went ahead and gave him the anointing and sealing ordinance. When I lifted my hands from his head and reached to take my Bible from his chest, the boy tightened his grip around the book. He would not let it go. And we left.

"Two days later we visited with the family again about the boy's condition. They reported that he was much improved. He had hugged that Bible all night. The family felt sorry that the Bible got soaked from the boy's incredible perspiration as the fever finally broke. But that book became even more valuable to me because of the boy's faith."

Jim flipped the pages to show our children the stained cover and sheets, allowing each child to handle his Bible. It had a profound effect on them.

During every scripture session, each member of our family took a turn reading a few verses from the selected scripture. Not to be left out, the toddler very soberly "read" a brief bit of baby jargon from his picture book. Of course, we flooded him with compliments. Then one day an amazing thing happened. He insisted on reading from my Bible. Apparently he had noticed how the siblings, who were beginning readers, moved a finger across the printed lines. This was to help them keep their place. Sitting on my lap, Tony put his tiny finger on the text in my Bible. When it was his turn to "read" he babbled his nonsense. Suddenly he said, "Jesus!" and pointed to that sacred name in print. Maybe he recognized the letters he had seen in his baby book. Surely something clicked in his mind. Whatever else it was to this child not yet two years old, he miraculously had caught on to reading, which was about symbols the mind recognized to stir the soul. And "Jesus" was his first experience with recognizing truth through the scriptures!

It was a high moment, a memory repeated for our youngest child as he grew up and was ordained a deacon, honored at a missionary farewell, a wedding shower, and then, too soon, a funeral when he was only forty-two and the father of three. Tony's epitaph was one of his favorite scriptures, and surely appropriate for him as a competing Boston Marathon runner: "Thy word is a lamp unto my feet, and a light unto my path" (Psalm 119:105).

When Jim died, exactly a year after our youngest child had died, we chose for his epitaph: "Experiment upon the word" adapted from Alma's sermon to the Zoramites: "But behold, if ye will awake and arouse your faculties, even to an experiment upon my words, and exercise a particle of faith, yea, even if ye can no more than desire to believe, let this desire work in you, even until ye believe in a manner that ye can give place for a portion of my words" (Alma 32:27).

Always concerned that our children might not fully understand the gospel and the value of applying it to life from one's earliest days, Jim engaged us in a challenging plan. Each week he would put a new scripture on the family bulletin board. For fifty-two weeks a year, each of us was to try, in a particularly committed way, to apply that scripture to daily life, to "experiment upon the word." It would be a good idea, he said, for those who could write even a bit, to jot down feelings and findings on an index card. At the end of the week we'd discuss the results during family home evening. As it turned out, only the head of our home made little notes every week on the cards he always carried in his left shirt pocket. At family report time, a chorus of excuses would rise up from the children, "But I don't have a pocket in my shirt to carry the card!" That memory always triggers laughter to this day.

At year's end, we knew we had benefited from experimenting upon the word, but only the father in the family had the makings for a best-selling book prepared from the accumulated notes! That book of fifty-two essays was published and titled, *Mormon Essays—An Experiment Upon the Word*. It was a hit beyond our family. Many readers were moved to try the experiment—to try marching to the same drummer as Nephi, Alma, King Benjamin, Helaman, Ether, Moroni, and Mormon. The biggest reward from Jim's effort was in the spiritual maturity we noticed in our growing youngsters. Now that they are parents themselves each has expressed gratitude for more than the examples of their mom and dad. They value the habit of scripture study, and as we have visited their homes we have been more than ready to take a turn in their family scripture study. In one family there is only one child left in the home, James Cannon McOmber. To bring a feeling of closeness to this young grandson, he sits in the middle of the big bed in the master bedroom while we kneel around it. Our scriptures are open before us on the bed for out-loud reading and discussion before family prayer.

Being educated in the scriptures, children grow in readiness and acceptance—most of the time—to abide the self-discipline, to reason out life's choices using eternal principles, to consider the Ten Commandments and the Beatitudes as valid standards in today's world, and to understand the steps to repentance.

When the way gets hard for me, I think again about the scripture that reminds us that comfort comes "by study and also by faith" (D&C 109:7).

Unless scripture study is the *family* pattern, trying to guide each other through contemporary Babylon and heartbreak is nigh impossible. It was true for our family when we were young parents, and it is true today for our children who are now parents with problems of their own. Everything changes, but nothing changes. If it were not so, family life would be like watching pro-football all New Year's Day with guests who don't understand the plays. Dismal. A parent might as well be speaking Farsi to the family or quoting Shakespeare to a group of kindergartners. They just don't get what you want them to.

I am not just talking about children obeying the family rules, or strictly keeping the Word of Wisdom, but, as well, living "by every word that proceedeth forth from the mouth of God" (D&C 84:44). Life is increasingly better when it is based on adherence to higher gospel principles. Blessings flow to a family as, gradually by precept and example, they learn to live by the first and great commandment and the significant second one which is like unto the first. It is about loving and testifying of Christ in thought and deed, and loving Heavenly Father's other children with as high esteem as He holds us. It is about respectful, kind behavior toward each other.

The following family event illustrates my point. It was the morning of Christmas Eve, and I took a phone message for our high school son who was working. The caller was a young man asking if Tony could work for him that night, Christmas Eve. They were busboys at a very fine local restaurant.

When Tony came home, I passed the message along.

He balked. Christmas was his favorite time.

I mentioned true Christmas spirit.

Enough already. He had just finished working and was exhausted. I was ruining his day.

I urged that it would be a nice gift to give someone in need.

He flatly refused and went to his room.

(The trouble with today's housing is that everyone has "a room" to hide in. Surely rearing children was easier when everyone mixed in the hogan, the tent, the igloo, the pioneer cabin, or the tract house.)

Actually, I didn't want Tony to miss the Christmas Eve family gathering either, but the other boy had a very good excuse for needing a substitute. Besides, this seemed an opportunity to discover the true meaning of Christmas. Also, I knew there would be times ahead in Tony's life when personal sacrifice would *have* to be made whether it was Christmas Eve or not. Learning how to function in a life of service to others seemed better learned sooner than later, since a mission call awaited him in another year or so.

I consulted the scriptures. Bearing one another's burdens is part of the covenant of baptism. It was God's idea and not mine, this was not just a family by-law. God clearly supports that "do unto others as you would have them do unto you" is a golden rule of human relationships and happiness. I went to his room, knocked, and walked right in, Bible in hand. Tony was resting on his bed with his back to the door. Touching him gently on the shoulder, I said his name in love, for I did love this youngest son. He grunted, which was a clue that he was alert enough to hear the beautiful lines on love which I read from Matthew 22:39. "Thou shalt love thy neighbor as thyself." I asked, "What do you think? We could juggle dinner and the program so you could also help your neighbor, so to speak."

Grunt, groan.

"Does that mean you want me to call him back and strike a deal for a split shift? One works early and the other takes the late shift, you know, do unto others. Then each of you could pick up some of the Christmas spirit. Okay?"

"Okay. Okay. O-KAY!"

Still, he did not roll over to look me in the eye. But I turned the stereo volume up so that "Oh, Come, All Ye Faithful" resounded into his room. He did go back to work, and he came home later liking himself (and me) better. That is a spin-off of following God's user manual for humans moving through the plan of life.

To illustrate further, we called the sunny room on our second floor the Mole Hole. It was the place where the women of the family (who outnumbered the men) became buried in projects like laundry duty, hair styling and drying, poster painting for school and church visuals, and family needs requiring the sewing machine. Great "girl talk" happened here, too. But one busy day (at the peak of my parenting years) this Mole Hole was the scene of a crushing blow to my self-esteem as the mother in a gospel-oriented family.

I sat at the sewing machine preoccupied with a rush job of stitching a skirt for a daughter who was experiencing her first season working away from home. Suddenly I realized her younger sister was leaning against the door frame watching me. When she noted my attention she flung these burning words at me, "Mom, why are you always sewing for Kiki and never for me?" I heard the sob before she disappeared.

I was stunned. Our uncomplaining young teenager was complaining. Our competent seamstress was being incompatible.

My martyr's day complex heightened.

My immediate reaction was to tangle my guiding finger with the sewing machine needle. The pain was severe and I matched it to her uneasy heart—which must have been uneasy and pained or she never would have blurted out such jealous words. She wouldn't dare question my motives so rudely. But she had dared! A teaching moment was at hand, if only I could think what to say.

My second reaction was just as automatic. I prayed, "Which of Heavenly Father's principles will help me now?"

I put my mind on seek and search. With which absolute from the word of God could I appease my beloved youngest daughter? How could I help her to understand that, indeed, each disappointment in life has a remedy in the scriptures.

Still praying, I went into her room, put an arm about her shoulders, and reminded her of Christ's parable of the prodigal son. The key players were the errant son, the jealous older brother, and the understanding father. Then I likened the biblical cast to our own family. I further explained that this was a type of the forgiving Heavenly Father shows us when we make mistakes.

"I am sewing for Kiki because she needs help right now. But—" I paused a moment—"do you have any idea how much I love you because I *don't* have to sew for you? Tired mother that I am, I am grateful you are one skilled seamstress and I am proud of you."

I went back to my sewing machine. In a few minutes she came to me with the idea that she could prepare a care package of goodies for her sister that could include the skirt I was stitching. Again I was thankful for the scriptures which had provided common ground for seeing, comprehending, and healing.

The truth is, that when you look for a scripture to solve a certain problem, you find so many wonderful thoughts on a variety of other subjects that hope wipes out worry. On the other hand, there is one scripture that fills my heart with sadness when people do not live by scriptural standard. It is the setting where the Nephites had become a sinful and warring people and wanted Mormon to lead them, one more time, against their enemies the Lamanites. In response, Mormon took *all* the precious records and buried them against destruction. Finally he agreed to lead their forces forth. "But behold," he records, "I was without hope, for I knew the judgments of the Lord which should come upon them; for they repented not of their iniquities, *but did struggle for their lives without calling upon that Being who created them*" (Mormon 5:2; emphasis added).

Let it not be said of us that we were so foolish as to not get help from our Creator, who, according to his own word, is waiting to be gracious to us. Seeking and learning of God and his purposes "by study and also by faith" (D&C 109:7) is the way to successfully deal with life's most traumatic challenges.

During my husband's long, final illness we still studied the scriptures together. We pleasured in the word of God by noting language, symbolism, parallelism, and finding a chiasmus or a coincidence. When Jim could no longer take a turn reading, he chose the scripture, and I would remind him of when he had used the scripture in a talk, a funeral address, or an essay. He would smile and nod at the memory. Even the memory of a scripture experience was a lovely thing in a life however narrowed by circumstance. When I read the scriptures out loud, I read with as much beauty of expression as my language-loving mother would approve. I also read to her before she died. I was amazed that though she was too weak to open her eyes, she followed the text intently. If I paused a moment to get my breath or perhaps to test if she were sleeping, Mother would pick up where I left off, complete the Article of Faith, recite the rest of a phrase in 3 Nephi 17, or complete the paragraph in the History of Joseph Smith. She had been an apt scholar of the scriptures in word and in living.

Sometimes our list of anguish was longer than usual. Often it included the special needs of friends and loved ones. We learned another truth: with a pile-up of problems God has our full attention, so we learn more. We search the scriptures. We search our own souls for signs of unworthiness or the need to repent—have we been slow to hearken unto the voice of the Lord our God? This stunning scripture inevitably comes to mind when our need is great *now*: "In the day of their peace they esteemed lightly my counsel; but, in the day of their trouble, of necessity they feel after me" (D&C 101:8).

We repeatedly value the wisdom of giving serious consideration *all the time* to the laws "irrevocably decreed in heaven before the foundations of this world, upon which all blessings are predicated" (D&C 130:20).

The longer I live the clearer the vision becomes of how God's plan for us is peppered with a variety of trials to push us to our limit, either by the nature of the problem, the cost of it, or the unrelenting assault of all kinds of struggles. When the ultimate grief strikes—and when it strikes again and then again—it is a wake-up call to look for the lesson and learn!

I went through a close series of deaths, which took both of my brothers, my daughter, my son, and my husband in a tight period of time. Meanwhile, for a season, I fought for my own life. Along the way, through the illness, the dying, and the deaths, I discovered Mosiah 24:13–16. It was a neon-light moment. That is a scripture to share, to reapply to yet another type of trial. Alma and his people were in deep anguish and so great were their afflictions because of their enemy that they did not only "raise their voices to the Lord their God, but did pour out their hearts to him; and he did know the thoughts of their hearts" (v. 12). What solace that sentence brings! The story unfolds, "And it came to pass that the voice of the Lord came to them in their afflictions, saying: Lift up your heads and be of good comfort . . . and I will also ease the burdens which are put upon your shoulders, that even you cannot feel them upon your backs" (vv. 13–14).

This promise worked for me. I did not feel the burden of being an ill woman who was at once slave laborer, caregiver, and cheerleader to loved ones in need. If they did it in the Book of Mormon, I could do as much in my day of crying out. Besides, I could go to bed between clean sheets laundered in my spiffy spinner.

But there was more that I learned, thanks be to Heavenly Father.

The Lord strengthened Alma's people, and He counseled them to stand as witnesses for Him that it would be known abroad that He does visit His people in their afflictions (see v. 14). Also, we His people, are to submit "cheerfully and with patience to all the will of the Lord" (v. 15).

The positive marching orders "lift up your heads, be of good comfort," and the assurance that the pain would be over because the dear Lord would get involved, has helped me again and again. I cannot begin to express the smallest part of what I feel in gratitude to the Lord for such scriptures, which give us particular access to Him.

We know that regardless of the setting of a scripture, God's words are meant for all of us, and He confirms those words.

By assignment from Church leadership, my life has been rich with opportunities to study, prepare, and teach the eternal principles of the gospel. President Harold B. Lee, the moving force behind priesthood correlation, taught us in the first Correlation

Committee meetings that no program or idea should be brought forth that was not based upon scripture. Each suggestion, however carefully considered, was to be considered invalid unless it had a scriptural basis. Over long years of participating in the various committee meetings I have been a witness to such wisdom. Repeatedly, the focus has been to get the members to study the scriptures for themselves. As this pattern is followed, teachers, leaders, and parents, became increasingly humble and quicker in seeking the Lord's counsel through His word.

Another powerful lesson regarding the value of the scriptures in life, occurred one dawn as I sneaked down a hall in my daughter Holly's Seattle home to listen behind a half-open door as she taught teenagers in early morning seminary. They read from the Book of Mormon; they responded to questions with chapter and verse; they shared personal perspectives. I was tenderly aware of a wonderful, strong Spirit in that basement room. Tears filled my eyes as I admitted (to myself) one more time, that in scripture study one can come so close to the Lord it is as if He is speaking Himself. These young people from scattered places and mixed religious affiliation, were being trained up in the way they should go.

In the early Church there was a "season of joy," so-called when the first missionary elders began returning to Nauvoo from their labors abroad. The Prophet Joseph assured them that the Spirit of the Lord enlightens men, but the world lies in sin. Therefore, the Saints were to continue testifying of these things, and if the people rejected them, then, said the Lord, "The hour of their judgment is nigh, and their house shall be left unto them desolate" (D&C 84:115). No matter how painful the demands of life, may our homes never be left desolate!

It becomes incredibly important that we get this information to act upon. I like the meaning of the word *train*. By specialized instruction or focus to cause or shape (a plant, one's hair, or a child) to take a desired course. No matter what else happens in life, peace can be ours if we are trained to live by God's word and His will.

When we trust in the Lord, learn His word and live by His will, we shall not be confounded, nor shall a fallen hair go unnoticed. The Lord has said that by doing these things, "the gates of hell shall not prevail against [us] . . . the Lord God will disperse the powers of darkness from before [us], and cause the heavens to shake for [our] good" (D&C 21:6). Unimaginable blessings will be ours, not because we are good but because God is. And that is a prize of a life lived according to His word. Surely that is the value in training up a child in the way he should go, as my mother did to prepare my heart for the sacrament service so long ago.

NOTES

1. Joseph Smith, as quoted by John Taylor in *Millennial Star,* 13:339.

CHAPTER 12

THE SACRED WORD OF GOD TO WHICH WE OWE ALL OUR HAPPINESS

Marion D. Hanks

As I was writing this essay, a telephone call came from one of our strong missionaries from Britain of more than thirty-five years ago. He and his wife had been blessed with a little girl who in her early years was stricken with leukemia. There was little hope for her recovery, but friends and family rallied to their support, and good medical help—strengthened by faith and prayers and fasting and earnest priesthood blessings—brought sweet results, and she outgrew the threatening illness. For their part the parents sought and received understanding and support through thoughtful reading and pondering of the scriptures.

The telephone call that day was prompted, our friends told us, by a feeling that lessons we had learned together in England about searching the scriptures had led to reassuring faith. "We read only the scriptures," the husband testified, "not books

Marion D. Hanks is an emeritus General Authority, receiving his call in 1953. He has served as a President of the Seventy, executive director of the Priesthood Department of the Church, president of the Salt Lake Temple, and president of the British Mission. He is the author of Bread Upon the Waters, The Gift of Self, *and* Now and Forever. *He is married to the former Maxine Christensen, and they are the parents of five children.*

explaining the scriptures; and we were led to spiritual truths that we found remarkable, full of comfort and hope."

The missionary, knowing nothing of this essay, had a strong urge to call us, after a long period of being out of touch, to share his family's joy over their experience with the scriptures. His telephone call supplied yet another helpful witness of the conviction I desire to express here: the scriptures are filled with wonderful strength and comfort and exist to teach us and guide us, individually and as families.

The testimony of those grateful parents recalls the experience of Paul and Silas who were driven from Thessalonica to Berea where they found the people "were more noble than those in Thessalonica, in that they received the word with all readiness of mind, and searched the scriptures daily, whether those things were so" (Acts 17:11). Our friends had also searched the scriptures with readiness to receive, and were deeply blessed.

The method of studying the scriptures recalled with such enthusiasm by our former missionary and his family is one I have enjoyed over a lifetime of teaching the scriptures. I commend it to your consideration.

* * *

Soon after I returned home from overseas service in the United States Armed Forces in World War II in 1945, I was invited to teach an early morning class at the LDS seminary across the street from the high school from which I had graduated. This schedule permitted me to spend a pleasant forty-five minutes each morning learning from the scriptures together with bright, interested young men and women before I drove to classes at the law school where I was enrolled.

I remembered my own final seminary year with appreciation. My teacher at that time was a lawyer who loved teaching the gospel and did it warmly and well. Wartime and its aftermath had beckoned him, at least for a time, back to the classroom where he could share with choice young people his reinforced convictions about the values and virtues the Church and gospel teach us to bless our lives. We were fortunate to have this strong instructor whose example influenced me to consider following a path similar to his. Now, here I was, back in the classroom after my own war experience, and eager to bless the lives of young Latter-day Saints as he had blessed mine.

One day early in this teaching experience I was invited to visit with the commissioner of education for the Church. We had not met previously, and I was pleased as he mentioned favorable reports he had received about my seminary class. As we finished the interview he expressed an interest in my teaching methods and wanted to hear my report about a still-earlier class underway each morning at the seminary.

I explained to him that I had been approached several weeks into the term by a group of students who asked if there were anything I could do to help them graduate from seminary. They were all outstanding young people, so active in school leadership and extracurricular programs that their activities had so filled their schedules that they had too few seminary credits to qualify for graduation.

I told them I was very interested in helping them but didn't know what could be done under the circumstances. "Unless," I said with a twinkle in my eye, "you would like to come at six in the morning. We might be able to arrange another class at that hour."

Without hesitation, they replied, "OK!" and the class was born, in concept at least. But would they really come at that hour in the morning in what was reported to be the most blizzardy winter in recorded Utah history?

Their answer was *yes*, but would they come consistently and endure to the end?

I told Commissioner West that day that such devotion in these high-quality young people deserved a warm response, and he agreed.

"But will they come?" he asked.

"To this date, remarkably, yes," I answered, and explained

that about forty students were in attendance each morning and more were inquiring about attending.

The young people wanted to study the Book of Mormon. I had agreed, and before the first meeting had acquired inexpensive copies of the book for all students. Each student received a book inscribed to him or her. Copies of the other standard works of scripture were available in the seminary library. We would teach from the scriptures themselves and were already launched from the first day in that procedure. So the Book of Mormon was the basic text each day, and all references in the class were to the Book of Mormon and the other standard works. As they wished, the students entered into the margins of their own sets of scriptures, notes, cross-references, other citations, and sources linking the subject matter.

At first I had done the reading and explaining, calling on students to read verses or passages and to comment or ask questions, as they desired. During the reading I referred them to other scriptures for supportive or explanatory purposes.

Commissioner West said, "You mean you stand and read from the book every day?"

"Yes."

"The students won't come," he said.

"But they do," I answered just as firmly. "In these weeks there have been few absences. Someone may go home ill with influenza, but the next morning he or she will break trail through the snow from California Avenue or Redwood Road to the seminary and be there on time."

"I don't understand that," he said.

"It's the book, the spirit of it, the 'likening' of its important teachings to their own immediate lives," I said. "And I grew up in that area. I know many of their families. They begin quickly to respond to the book."

He was still shaking his head. He then wanted to know what specific objectives we were pursuing. And was there a structure or format for learning consistently followed?

Yes to both questions.

I had used the same process with my family, study groups, in firesides and in the mission field, and, when I had occasion ashore as an authorized Church group leader, in teaching various gatherings of LDS personnel. I had followed my simple "Steps to Learning" and the Nephi "purposes of scripture" instructions from 1 Nephi 19:22–24. I had found his objectives to be effective with any volume of scripture in appropriately exposing the book to those who were not familiar with it.

Recently I received a letter from a student in those first morning classes who had later enjoyed a successful career in Church employment as secretary to several of the Brethren. She had retired early to help care for a grandchild who needed full-time attention because of a medical problem. She was now serving as a stake Relief Society president, and, with her husband, as an ordinance worker in the temple.

As a high school girl, she had come to that early morning class with a troubled heart, almost fearing to hear the lessons she was sure would further emphasize her anxieties. Her letter referred to a talk I had delivered which had been recently replayed over KBYU television:

> I somehow always return in memory to so many testimony beginnings in the West High Seminary building. We often sang, "Truth Reflects upon Our Senses" or "I Stand All Amazed," two of my favorites to this day. You occasionally furnished breakfast goodies as we arose so early to attend. The Book of Mormon could not have had a better introducer for me. The Book of Mormon characters and the vocabulary were instilled in a very special way. My parents had divorced and my father had remarried—neither marriage under the covenant. I longed for that "belonging" but you gave the precious answer (I am certain under direct inspiration) that sometimes we could step forward and be a "beginning," making certain we were obedient and worthy to have the covenants for our children. I knew I could have that eternal family I longed for. Because of the wonder of hearts turning, I was able to

do the temple work for my parents and hear those wonderful words, "as if you had been born in the covenant." How I have treasured that sweet motivation you gave throughout my life. It really happened.

Over the years I have received many other kind expressions of encouragement from people responding to this approach to teaching the sacred books from a background of understanding of their own personal lives and needs, with their energetic participation in marking and annotating their books.

* * *

The recitation of the sentence which begins the Book of Mormon and is probably as well known as any scripture in the book should be read in class as written. But the students' knowledge of the circumstances is needed to make that sentence come alive. Nephi explains, immediately following the opening words, what he means by being "born of goodly parents": "therefore, I was taught somewhat in all the learning of my father" (1 Nephi 1:1). He sets the stage for all attentive fathers, though not all have understood or played their parts well. Some questions immediately come to mind:

- Why should Nephi be grateful for his parents?
- What obligation did they have to him and his siblings?
- Did they fulfill their responsibilities to Nephi and the others?
- What did Nephi and the other children owe them?
- How could the children repay them?
- What if our parents are not keeping the commandments?
- What obligation do we have to parents who do not seem to qualify as "goodly parents" under Nephi's declaration?

Each of us owes a debt to our parents, to the fathers and mothers of our faith, our freedom, our mortal bodies, for life itself, and for such gifts of love and kindness and care as were offered along the way.

This is the issue to which the writer of the letter directed her remarks so forcefully. Unable as a girl to connect currently with her own parents, she had learned that she could "step forward and be a beginning."

The commissioner wanted to know what we were doing for lesson outlines. I said, "I organize them as we go."

So, in the class, I explained study objectives and class structure and frequently referred to them. The scriptures themselves have many helpful suggestions of purpose in reading and pondering, but perhaps the simplest and clearest and most useful are those announced in 1 Nephi 19:22–25.

In these verses Nephi offered an explanation for his reading from the brass plates to his people: "I [Nephi] did read many things to them, which were engraven upon the plates of brass, that they might know concerning the doings of the Lord in other lands, among the people of old" (v. 22).

That is, Nephi wanted his people to know the history of God's dealings with them through prophets in other times and other places. For example, Moses in Exodus 19:9: "And the Lord said unto Moses, Lo, I come unto thee in a thick cloud, that the people may hear when I speak with thee, and believe thee forever."

> And I did read many things unto them which were written in the book of Moses; but that I might more fully persuade them to believe in the Lord their Redeemer I did read unto them that which was written by the prophet Isaiah. (v. 23)

He wanted them to come to a testimony of Jesus. Among the prophets, Isaiah was especially blessed with a vision of the birth, life, mission, atoning love, suffering, passion, death, resurrection, and eternal place with His Father of the Savior Jesus Christ. With repeated reference to the writings of Isaiah, Nephi declared the ultimate purpose of learning the truth and gaining a testimony of Christ, "for I did liken all scriptures unto us, that it might be for our profit and learning" (v. 23).

The full value of any scripture can be understood only when we know and understand previous instructions and guidance from the Lord to His people, have a testimony of Jesus and the gospel, and then apply the lessons and commandments in our own lives!

This last reason for teaching the scriptures to his people Nephi repeated again as recorded in verse 24: "hear ye the words of the prophet, which were written unto all the house of Israel, and liken them unto yourselves, that ye might have hope as well as your brethren."

What are the steps to learning that can bring us these blessings? Looking always to the objectives, those whom we teach must be brought to:

Read. We know that "those who will not read are no better off than those who cannot"; in fact, they may be worse off because of attitude or apathy. Scores of instructions concerning scripture study can be found all through the sacred books.

Listen. King Benjamin instructed his people that they should "hearken . . . and open your ears that you may hear, and your hearts that you may understand, and your minds that the mysteries of God may be unfolded to your view" (Mosiah 2:9).

Mark. Assemble, collect, cross-reference, outline, underline, make notes, block out, shade, point out, point up, and link.

Ponder, meditate, think. Writes Nephi: "As [my Father] read [the scriptures], he was filled with the Spirit of the Lord" (1 Nephi 1:12). What a precious, indispensable blessing to a faithful seeker of truth!

At the conclusion of the momentous day at the temple in the land of Bountiful, the Savior told the people to "go ye unto your homes, and ponder upon the things which I have said, and ask of the Father, in my name, that ye may understand, and prepare your minds for the morrow" (3 Nephi 17:3). After pondering and praying about what they had heard and felt, they would undertake to

Digest. "So they read in the book in the law of God distinctly, and gave the sense, and caused them to understand the reading" (Nehemiah 8:8).

Liken, apply—faithfully. Nephi, on reading to his family the words of Isaiah, "did liken all scriptures unto us . . . for our profit and learning" (1 Nephi 19:23).

Deuteronomy 6:3—"Hear . . . observe to do it."

Deuteronomy 31:12—"Hear, . . . learn, and fear the Lord your God."

Mosiah 4:10—"If you believe all these things see that ye do them."

Share generously, serve, give. Ezra 7:10— "Seek the law of the Lord, . . . do it, . . . teach in Israel."

Deuteronomy 6:7—"And thou shalt teach them diligently unto thy children, and shalt talk of them when thou sittest in thine house, and when thou walkest by the way, and when thou liest down, and when thou risest up."

Each of these steps to learning is fully amplified by many instructions in the standard works and leads students to living, believing, and serving in the work of the Lord.

After more than twenty years of teaching in Church classes, and after nearly fifty years of marriage and children, with many years of traveling the earth in Church leadership, I am more than satisfied that there is no greater or more rewarding work than teaching the study of the scriptures and observing in some measure the effect of that pleasant undertaking.

* * *

And our experience in teaching the holy scriptures in our own home to our own family has been wonderfully rewarding. The gentle Martin Buber taught us that "Our greatest treasure is hidden beneath the hearth in our own home."

Sister Hanks and I have reveled in this treasure, which has been, for our family, the discovery of our human responsibilities to be charitable to our neighbors, to treat them as ourselves. We learned together that the heart of the scriptural message is to cultivate charity toward all people. What a vital lesson for families to apply in their lives!

As I prepared this essay, I bravely asked our five children to speak candidly of their remembered times at home as we studied, books open, around a table, with everyone participating. Their responses were humbling and encouraging. "We didn't understand everything when we were little," they said, "but the books were opened to us, for us, and became ours, the people 'made real.' We really didn't understand then that we were gaining a deep repository of habit and attitude, as well as knowledge and feeling, from which we could draw when it was time." Our young missionary grandchildren have joined in this appraisal. At the time of this conversation four of them were teaching Gospel Doctrine classes in their wards. The essence of what our family has found in the scriptures is that faith begets charity.

My family members tell me

> The "liken them to yourselves" experiences we had have never been forgotten. Who can measure the meaning and impact of the frozen winter nights when we were bundled in an old four-wheeler and driven a block to First South above University and the steep road below, to help, with our chains or rope, pull the cars stuck on the icy streets or against the curbs, some involved in accidents and others immobilized. We remember too that quite a few of them needed the use of a telephone and were welcomed for that purpose in our home, and for the warm soup Mom always had available on such occasions. Can any blessings be more glorious than those promised to those who cultivate charity?

Our family links the experiences of charitable service to the wonderful story in Alma chapters 17–20 concerning Ammon, a great missionary who won a place in the heart of the king and kingdom for his faithful service in the fields, resisting the enemies of the king and preserving his flocks, then staying on the job tending the horses while the award ceremonies were being held.

That same Ammon has become a kind of prototype of and example for nearly 60,000 missionaries across the earth. Each of them by direction of the Church leaders spends half a day or more each week in community or Christian service. For the past ten or eleven years, starting in 1988 and 1989, full-time LDS missionaries in southeast Asia have been working in border camps doing the work of Christ among a suffering group of refugees from several countries who fully meet the description of the Savior in his parable of the judgment recorded in Matthew 25:31–46. Those whom the King blessed by bidding them to "inherit the kingdom prepared for you from the foundation of the world" (v. 34) were so honored because they had cared for the needs of the Lord when he was hungry, thirsty, homeless, naked, sick, and in prison.

The honest Saints gathered at his right hand declared their unworthiness to receive the blessing conferred by the Lord because they could not recall ever seeing the Lord in the circumstances he described, and helping him: "When saw we thee an hungered and fed thee? or thirsty and gave thee drink?" they ask the Lord. "When saw we thee a stranger, and took thee in? or naked, and clothed thee? Or when saw we thee sick, or in prison, and came unto thee?" (vv. 37–39). Every family enjoying scripture study should be able to repeat in unison the answer the Lord gave to this group of his unselfish Saints: "Inasmuch as ye have done it unto one of the least of these my brethren, ye have done it unto me" (v. 45).

To those who had not responded to the needs of others, who had not developed the habit of helpfulness, had not learned the principle of unselfish service, Christ spoke harsh words as he bade them "go away into everlasting punishment," while the righteous went on "into life eternal" (v. 46).

It was fascinating to observe that the missionaries serving for six to eight months in the refugee camps of Asia—encouraging and teaching these suffering people, helping them to prepare for life in the United States or other third-world countries—operated under dangerous conditions and kept very demanding work schedules without complaint. They completed their period of assignment in the camps and, without exception, characterized their experiences with these thoughts, often in these words: "This was the most decent thing I have ever done. My life will never be the same."

We have been most grateful to observe that families who have studied together the powerful scriptural admonitions of the Lord and followed His holy pattern of selfless service and sacrifice, likening the principles unto themselves, are blessed with unparalleled joy.

The observation of President J. Reuben Clark of the First Presidency in general conference in April 1937 is a warmly received declaration of compassionate concern which leads to active involvement in helping those who have need of help among our fellowmen:

> When the Savior came upon the earth he had two great missions; one was to work out the Messiahship, the atonement for the fall, and . . . the other was the work which he did among his brethren and sisters in the flesh by way of relieving their sufferings . . . . He left as a heritage to those who should come after him in his Church the carrying on of those two great things—work for the relief of the ills and sufferings of humanity, and the teaching of the spiritual truths which should bring us back into the presence of our Heavenly Father.[1]

Indeed, Christ's "work for the relief of the ills and the sufferings of humanity" stands on par with His Saviorhood and Atonement! This great statement is totally consistent with the countless declarations in the scriptures testifying that service to God and our fellowmen in the gospel plan is not "optional" after we have taken care of the other fundamental instructions of our faith, but is of equal power and importance to any of them.

A similar burden is laid upon the faithful Saints in the great sermon of Amulek in Alma 34 where we are taught to pray over all the circumstances of our lives, and then, "do not suppose that this is all; for after ye have done all these things, if ye turn away the needy, and the naked, and visit not the sick and afflicted, and impart of your substance, if ye have, to those who stand in need—I say unto you, if ye do not any of these things, behold, your prayer is vain, and availeth you nothing, and ye are as hypocrites who do deny the faith" (Alma 34:28).

I also received a note from one of our children with a long memory who wrote:

> In our family, all of us remember many stops at the roadside to help people in trouble, using equipment carried along always in the station wagon or four-wheeler for that purpose. Hospital visits and homes-of-widows visits were understood to be part of our regimen, but when the foundation was laid for the experience by reading the relevant scriptures, all of that became very personal and very basic, as they are now in our own families.

Another of our children who has manifested a consistent, long-term sense of responsibility for the downtrodden, the immigrant, the refugee families wrote:

> We have had so many interesting people visit our home from far-away places, and so many remember and remind us in letters of their association with our family that we can draw on the memories to help us as we teach our children and others in our home, in classes, in family home evenings, missionary farewell preparations, etc.
>
> We remember so well Donna and Susannah and Violet, all pseudonyms for ladies who stayed in our home with us for varying periods of time. Susannah was with us during the Christmas season one year when she was separated from her husband and children and had been in an institution until a few days before Christmas. You found her when you were responsible for Temple Square, and brought her home.

Our daughter recalls one of our happiest Christmas seasons because we had a wonderful, typical family celebration on Christmas Eve, with presents and participation for everyone. Susannah, like each person staying with us in our home, took part in the singing, reading of scriptures, and traditional treasured stories accumulated over the years; and in prayers. Then, because she seemed stable and so much better, we called her family on Christmas morning and learned how anxious they were to have her home, so that was arranged and she arrived there in time to celebrate with her family. We received word that she remained happily well thereafter, and for a long time we kept in touch.

Our daughter continues:

> Violet's story was similar, except she was a convert carrying a baby, without a husband, and she was bitter, even though Mom had volunteered to give her a home while the baby was preparing to arrive, then went with her to the hospital to bring the child into the world. Our mother treated her as if she were one of her own children and watched her attitude change when she learned she really was accepted and really loved and cared for. Dad, in his frequent travels, met Violet several times thereafter in various places, including stake conferences, at airline counters, etc., when she had developed a stable family and Church life.
>
> With this background and blessing in our lives, none of us needed much of a detailed explanation of what is meant by our responsibility to those who are "hungry, thirsty, naked, homeless, sick, and in prison."

The great "jungle physician," Dr. Albert Schweitzer, serving in his isolated hospital in French Equatorial Africa, spoke to a group of young, able medical students who had come to Africa to see his work. He said, "I don't know what your destiny will be, but one thing I know: the only ones among you who will be truly happy are those who have sought and found how to serve."

***

In the story of Jacob at Bethel, when he awakened from his

dream of a ladder reaching to heaven, he said, "Surely the Lord is in this place; and I knew it not . . . . This is none other but the house of God, and this is the gate of heaven" (Genesis 28:16–17). In the scriptures a person can be lifted to a sense of reverence, a sense of appreciation for God, to know that wherever we are—in our homes, the hills, our centers of enterprise, in places of recreation—we can, according to our desires, our will, and our humility, qualify for that spiritual presence and power which will surely bring us the strength we need and the joy we desire. This requires that we appreciate that we are a little more than human, that we are related to Him who is much more than human; it requires that we remain open to an increasing sense of wonder and worship before His eternal holiness.

The blessing of familiarity with the scriptures is to share them and "liken them" to ourselves, to recall the warmth and wonder of God's holy plan which provided for a Savior for all of us, who through his love and mercy made our presently imperfect lives brim with the beautiful and wonderful promises of a God who "so loved [us] that he gave his only begotten Son, that whosoever should believe in him should not perish, but have everlasting life. For God sent not his Son into the world to condemn the world; but that the world through him might be saved" (John 3:16–17).

Members of the Church need the blessing of the Spirit of the Lord and the merciful example of the life of the Lord as found in the scriptures, which provide course-correcting admonitions for all of us. But we must find the time and make the effort to read them. I love a line from Shakespeare's *Julius Caesar*. Brutus stands over the body of his friend Cassius. Preparing for his last battle, and himself about to die, Brutus speaks of Cassius, and then to him: "Friends, I owe more tears / To this dead man than you shall see me pay." Then, "I shall find time, Cassius, I shall find time" (5.3.101–3).

The scriptures are literally filled with wonderful "lessons of life" which are reducible or capable of enlargement sufficient to meet our individual needs and desires. There is no commentary that can replace scripture. Just as I learned in those precious experiences teaching seminary years ago, and have learned again and again in my life, the scriptures, to our eternal blessing, testify of Him.

NOTES

1. J. Reuben Clark, Jr., in Conference Report, April 1937, p. 22.

CHAPTER 13

THE LIAHONA EXPERIENCE: GETTING DIRECTIONS THROUGH THE SCRIPTURES

Neal E. Lambert

When Lehi and his family had finished their preparations and were ready to set out from the Valley of Laman, the Near-Eastern wilderness and its challenges must have been a heavy burden on their hearts. Without much effort, one can imagine the thoughts of Lehi and Sariah, for instance, as they tried to sleep that last night before launching out on what they surely knew would be a many-years-long journey. The rustling sounds of their animals and the stirrings of their sleeping children must have driven home the fact that Jerusalem and the comfort it afforded was now far behind them. They must have worried about getting their family through the wilderness as any pilgrim or pioneer would do. How far would it be? and how long? Would there be food for the babies? Would there be food for

Neal E. Lambert is a professor of English at Brigham Young University, where he has served as coordinator of American Studies, associate academic vice president, and chair of the English Department. He has been a member of the Sunday School General Board, a stake president, and mission president of the North Carolina-Raleigh Mission. He edited, with Richard H. Cracroft, A Believing People: Literature of the Latter-day Saints, *and has published articles in the* New Era *and the* Ensign.

them? How would they organize the care and supervision of the subteens as they moved from camp to camp? Would there be more problems with the older boys? How would Ishmael's family and the new in-laws fit into their family patterns? And all this is to say nothing about cold nights, the heat of the day, storms, sickness, cuts, and scrapes. Would they encounter enemies or bandits or robbers in the unknown ahead of them? While the Lord had told them of their final destination in the land of promise, there were precious few instruction manuals about the day-to-day task of getting there.

As they lay in the darkness that morning, they must have sensed that the journey would not be easy. There would be countless campsites, and week after week after week of one-foot-after-the-other plodding, making slow progress through the gullies and hills and deserts of that wilderness. This was no "family special" in a 747 with helpful flight attendants to warm up the baby's bottle. This was an on-the-ground, through-the-dirt, over-the-rocks-and-brush, sand-in-the-sandals sort of expedition. They knew that it would be very, very hard, and so they must have been concerned a bit about their little ones, and about their not-so-little ones, and for themselves as well, as they considered the business of their extraordinary pilgrimage. If they awoke that last day with some degree of trepidation and anxiety, who could blame them. They had already suffered much and knew that the experiences of leaving Jerusalem and getting the plates and their returning for Ishmael and all the bruises and narrow escapes were only a prelude to what lay ahead.

Lehi and Sariah, however, were people of great faith and knew that the Lord would not leave them without direction and sustenance in the days ahead. They knew He could and would give them direction in the daily walk that made up the multiplying steps of their migration. And so on that important morning as Lehi arose, he "went forth to the tent door, [and] to his great astonishment he beheld upon the ground a round ball of curious workmanship; and it was of fine brass. And within the ball were two spindles; and the one pointed the way whither [they] should go into the wilderness" (1 Nephi 16:10). And, as Nephi explained further, "I, Nephi, beheld the pointers which were in the ball, that they did work according to the faith and diligence and heed which we did give unto them. And there was also written upon them a new writing, which was plain to be read, which did give us understanding concerning the ways of the Lord; and it was written and changed from time to time, according to the faith and diligence which we gave unto it" (1 Nephi 16:28–29).

That "understanding" covered not only doctrine, but it also included counsel for their everyday concerns. Even in the matter of obtaining food, for instance, Nephi was told to "go forth up into the top of the mountain, *according to the directions which were given upon the ball*" (1 Nephi 16:30; emphasis added). There is a wonderful ambiguity in that last phrase. Nephi does not say "*in the direction* which *was* given." Rather, he reports he went forth "*according to* the directions" given on the ball. Thus Nephi may well have followed not only the compass points which the spindles gave, but also the instructions about the manner in which he should go. Maybe the Lord told Nephi that if he would exercise faith and proceed prayerfully, it wouldn't matter which direction he went, and that the Lord would bring the food to him. That is speculation of course. But proceeding "according to the directions" must mean as much about prayer and fasting as it does about north and south.

We should never forget that the ball or compass or "director"—the Liahona, as it is called in other places, was essential to bringing Lehi and his family through their wilderness experience and landing them finally in the land of promise, not just because it pointed them east or north, but because it pointed them toward their God. It showed them where they could find good water and food, and it showed them as well where they could find their God. It was a constant reminder of the daily necessity of having the Lord's directing words before them. As a sign and token of such a principle, the Liahona was treasured by the descendants of Lehi, and, along with the sword of Laban and the Urim and Thummim, was still with the plates of the Book of

Mormon when Moroni gave them to Joseph Smith. As Alma the Younger explained in passing the records and the Liahona on to his own son centuries after Lehi had died:

> And now, my son, I would that ye should understand that these things are not without a shadow; for as our fathers were slothful to give heed to this compass (now these things were temporal) they did not prosper; even so it is with things which are spiritual.
>
> For behold it is as easy to give heed to the word of Christ, which will point to you a straight course to eternal bliss, as it was for our fathers to give heed to this compass, which would point unto them a straight course to the promised land.
>
> And now I say, is there not a type in this thing? For just as surely as this director did bring our fathers, by following its course, to the promised land, shall the words of Christ, if we follow their course carry us beyond this vale of sorrow into a far better land of promise.
>
> O my son, do not let us be slothful because of the easiness of the way; for so was it with our fathers; for so was it prepared for them, that if they would look they might live; even so it is with us. (Alma 37:43–46)

As Alma makes clear, the scriptures are our Liahonas. They are our directors for the trials and tribulations and challenges of our spiritual journey to which, if we will look, we can live. Like the Liahona, they sit in our "tent door"—by our beds, on our bookshelves, on our lamp stands and living room tables—waiting to be picked up and "looked unto." Our Liahonas are bound in black or brown or blue covers rather than made of fine brass. But the workmanship, as the footnotes, cross-references, map, dictionaries, gazetteers, and topical guides make impressively clear, is indeed "fine." And, if we will look, and "give heed," these pages, no less than the ball itself, can give daily direction for ourselves and for our families regarding the details of our own challenges in "making it through" this pilgrimage of life.

Recently I was myself suffering from a period of spiritual

insipidness and inspirational dullness. Sunday School preparations and planning an upcoming Book of Mormon course were necessary but insufficient remedies for the doldrums that seemed to drag on my soul like weights around my arms and legs. I suspected the cause: I hadn't been reading on a daily basis as I knew I should. Holiday visitors and family were welcome and wonderful guests, but along with the enjoyable demands and the different schedules of holiday activities, I really had done very little thoughtful and attentive reading in the scriptures, and I kept putting that need down deep into my ever-full daily to-do list. The effects were showing as the gloom of spiritual stagnation shadowed my soul.

In my struggle to revive my self, I sat down one morning, and, instead of opening to the usual Book of Mormon course material, passively let the pages of my old, well-worn triple combination fall open as they would. When I looked down, there on the right hand column were long familiar words from the book of Moses—the story of Adam and Eve and the angel's visitation to Adam as he makes sacrifices to the Lord. I had read these verses many times before, and taught them in Sunday School, in religion classes, and in zone conferences. But this time I seemed to be reading them for the first time. "And Adam and Eve, his wife, called upon the name of the Lord and they heard the voice of the Lord from the way toward the Garden of Eden, speaking unto them, and they saw him not; *for they were shut out from his presence*" (Moses 5:4; emphasis added). I, too, knew that the Lord was nearby, but I was painfully divided from Him, separated from the presence of His spirit in my own "dark and dreary waste" (1 Nephi 8:7).

Then I read on: "And he gave unto them commandments, that they should worship the Lord their God, and should offer the firstlings of their flocks, for an offering unto the Lord" (Moses 5:5). And "What," I asked myself, "has this to do with *my* worship and flocks? I am a busy college professor pressed by schedules and deadlines and demands and duties, not a quiet pastoral herdsman." And then in my mind I could see my great-great grandfather

Adam in the labor of his day: his hands grown calloused and hard from the work of making his own pots and tools, hands that were dirt-stained from the toil of planting, harvesting, and building. I could almost see the sweat dripping from his face and arms, as he labored, carrying and piling those uncut stones to build that altar—that first of many sacred places. The altar and its special labors must have become familiar to Adam, for he sacrificed there not once but for "many days," perhaps even for years. In time there must have been generations of sheep and goats and cattle feeding nearby, herds from which came milk and meat and cheese and skins and the all-important "firstlings" for sacrifice. And "after many days" there must have been as well and not too far away, children; Adam's own; born in a tent or under the open sky without sterile instruments and the professional direction of a learned OB-GYN, rather only with Adam's unlearned, inexperienced, and probably nervous hands assisting Eve in her labor as she "brought forth" those sons and daughters. Perhaps some of those children had even grown to be of a size to help, at least to wash and clean the selected animal, perhaps even leading the "firstling" to the altar where father Adam would preside in the sacrifice.

In all of this I sensed, that morning as I read, the bruising reality of living in the lone and dreary world outside the garden, a world with struggle and disappointment and pain and labor not all that different from my own. And how had Adam reacted? My eye went on to the next three words penciled onto the margin: "Absolute and Complete," written next to the line "And Adam was obedient unto the commandments of the Lord." Adam's reaction to his hard life was to be *absolutely and completely* obedient and faithful. Even when obedience was inconvenient or difficult, he obeyed; and perhaps more significantly, he did so in the face of not knowing the full reason why.

Going on now, and I confess, rather full of emotion, I read the angel's instructional query to Adam: "Why dost thou offer sacrifices unto the Lord?" and Adam's faith-filled response, "I know not, save the Lord commanded me" (Moses 5:6). Then I read the angel's profound and revelatory response to Adam: "This thing is a similitude of the sacrifice of the Only Begotten of the Father" (v. 7).

For years I had seen "this thing" simply as the lamb on the altar—the unblemished, firstborn little sheep—maybe struggling or bleating, innocent, white in color, perfect in form, ready for its life's blood to be shed, an effective symbol setting forth all the significance that Isaiah and others would give to "the Lamb of God." But now as I read "this thing," I could almost see the sweep of the angel's arm in an inclusive gesture that, while directing attention to the "firstling" on the altar, also pointed to the altar itself and all the physical effects of Adam's obedient life. Suddenly the meaning of "this thing" enlarged to become not a single sacrifice of a ewe's firstborn and unblemished lamb, but a multitude of smaller sacrificial acts in a compliant pattern of actions, a pattern of one man's daily self-sacrifice in an uncompromising, undeviating progress of obedience through many long days of devoted work and long-suffering, a self-sacrifice that was tied to and gave context to the lamb on the altar.

And then I saw another dimension to "this thing" in the remarkable way the Christ's own sacrificial life was reflected in the events that day at that first altar. For I saw in the pattern of Adam's obedience and sacrifice not only the Savior's spilled blood, but His many years of personal obedience and sacrifice, His days of labor and preparation and willing compliance and long-suffering and crucifixion. Thus, in my own dim way, I sensed and could see what I am sure the angel's words confirmed for Adam: that in his own obedience and sacrifice he was himself a likeness of the obedient Savior, that his (Adam's) life, was itself an acceptable offering not unlike the lamb lying before him in similitude upon the altar.

Then it seemed as though the angel turned to address me directly. "Wherefore, [Lambert]," I could hear him say, "thou shalt [be obedient like my other son Adam, and] do all that thou doest in the name of the Son, and thou [Neal] shalt repent and call upon God in the name of the Son forevermore." My challenge was clear: make my life more like Adam's and more like the Savior's.

As I pondered that morning, considering the needed spiritual adjustments for the days ahead, I went on to the next verse and read of the blessing that came to Adam. "And in that day the Holy Ghost fell upon Adam, which beareth record of the Father and the Son" (v. 9). And in that moment, the Holy Ghost fell upon my soul as well. My experience was not Adam's, but that morning reading these verses, I did feel the unmistakable "fire . . . in my bones" (Jeremiah 20:9), that stirring of spirit and the inspirational caress from outside myself, that confirming touch of the Lord's love and acceptance and assurance. Those verses that day dispelled my gloom, enlightened my heart, and gave me strength to continue through the tangle and steep hills of my own daily work.

I have learned over the years that even the physical presence of the scriptures can make a difference as a guide in our lives. Having the sacred texts physically at our fingertips can be almost like a spiritual life jacket when we feel ourselves drowning in the secular rivers of this fallen world, or smothered in the profanities of a spiritless environment. One beautiful young man I knew, a recent convert, was trying very hard to prepare for a mission, but he was working in surroundings flooded with filthy stories, cursing, swearing, and crude profanities. Carrying the scriptures with him on the job was out of the question, but he decided to keep loose pages of the Book of Mormon in his pocket, and in moments of intense frustration, take them out and read a few words, or at the very least put his hand on them, just to feel their presence and have the cleansing remembrance of what was on those pages—an antidote to the poisonous words around him. As he reported, that presence was a great saving help.

I remember as well visiting with a young woman who, having left home, perhaps prematurely, had allowed herself to drift with the currents of a life away from the Church. Her experiences had finally brought about the loss of her membership. But the depths of her sorrow never did drown her determination to work her way back. I shall never forget her inspiring image as we spoke about her future and her plans for repentance. "I know," she said, "that I no longer have the gift of the Holy Ghost." Then she picked up a blue-bound copy of the Book of Mormon and pressed it against her heart and said, "But I know I can still have the feelings from the Holy Ghost as I read in these pages." Her understanding of what the scriptures can do as a guide in our lives worked for her then and has since paid great dividends for her and those around her. For years now, she has been back serving in the Church and has held many teaching and leadership assignments, influencing in profound ways the young people she has taught and ministered to since those dark days.

As parents we may wonder sometimes whether the effort at regular scripture reading in the home is really worth the scrambles and troubles. Given the press of schedules and the sometimes conscious disinterest from people seated around the table, the task seems daunting. Every parent surely has experienced some of the mumbling grumbles and the studied boredom of teenagers, or the glassy-eyed unconsciousness of the nine- and ten-year-olds, or the distracting climbing up and down the furniture or the spoon pounding of the smallest toddlers. Surely we have each asked ourselves in these less-than-perfect family moments, "Is this really doing anybody any good?" Of course, in our hearts we know the answer even when that answer may never truly be evident until "after many days." But if we continue scripture reading in our homes, the Liahona experience will be there at those times when it is desperately needed. There will be times, perhaps years ahead, when a genuine surprise surfaces, a clear evidence of true spiritual penetration. I remember one such moment well.

We were sitting in a family council in the living room of a small house in central Massachusetts. Our little family, including our four youngest, had moved there during a sabbatical leave from Brigham Young University. My work was in Worcester, but the only accommodations we could afford for a family our size were in Dudley, one of the many small mill-towns scattered across the then less-than-prosperous countryside. The house was "different" in its arrangement, but we had accommodated ourselves to the one bathtub and sharing the half-bath with the washing machine. The unmistakably used furniture of the house still smelled of the nightclub that our landlord operated from which the piano and couches had already seen considerable service. Our little house was unusual, to say the least, but for our year away from home, it was doable.

Our family enjoyed many wonderful experiences together in New England, generally, and in the Worcester Ward in particular where we had an abundance of good times and good friends. Still, in the depth of that New England winter the anticipation of returning to our own comfortable home in Provo, Utah, was real. Before leaving the previous summer, our daughters had given last, longing looks at their bedrooms which they had just finished decorating. And during the intervening months they had talked more than once about having again closets and drawers for their own clothes, places for their pictures, shelves for their books, and enjoying again the friends and opportunities and comforts they had loved in the lives they left behind in Utah.

So our family council that January night was important and very serious. It concerned our return home. That day we had received a call from President Gordon B. Hinckley to serve for the next three years as mission president. We didn't yet know where, but we knew accepting the call would mean not returning to Provo next summer as we had planned. But our situation was more complicated than just postponing a return to our new house. We were in the middle of raising eight daughters, and our family expenses were at their highest point. Accepting the call might well mean having to sell our home. I explained as much to the family, so, as one might expect, the discussion was less than gleeful. As we talked over the possibilities and the implications for us, for our house—and for the bedrooms—I could see some chins quiver, and a few eyes brimmed with tears. Then our daughter Toni wiped her eyes and said, "Now I know how Laman and Lemuel felt. They just didn't want to leave their beautiful new home in Jerusalem."

There was a world of meaning in that response—for Toni, and for our family. It was clear that for her Laman and Lemuel were more than ciphers or story characters. They were real people in real-life situations. And those of us sitting there that night with Toni knew that she knew the record that told of *their* leaving home was true. Furthermore we knew that because the record was true, we would all, like Lehi and Nephi, "go and do," wherever and however the prophet called us. I don't know where Toni came to her testimony of Laman and Lemuel and Sam and Nephi and all the others in the Book of Mormon and the other scriptures. Whether or not it was in those seemingly futile mornings trying to do scriptures and cereal and sack lunches and car-pool arrangements before the family shot out through all the doors to their schools and practices and appointments, I couldn't really say. Certainly seminary and Sunday School had a good deal to do with it. But what matters is this: that night in Massachusetts, Toni knew, and we knew, even in the face of difficult choices, what we must do, and what we would do. To start that night a practice of family scripture reading would have been too late. On the day when it was crucial, the scriptural familiarity was there, and our Lambert Liahona-guide worked for Toni and for us all.

I firmly believe that the Lord is eager to bless us, to guide us, and to enlighten us in everything we do. That includes professional and recreational concerns as well as Church and family matters. We have all, at one time or another, been wonderfully surprised by finding in the scriptures just what we needed at the moment. A particular example, passage, or phrase has seemed precisely pertinent to a pressing need in our own situations, even when those situations may have seemed more "temporal" than "spiritual." This can happen as a continuous principle in our lives, but only if we are looking for that kind of direction, day by day. Only when we are actively involved in the pages of scripture can the Lord give us our "new writing," our own directions for our daily demands as he did Lehi and Nephi for theirs. An example from music may give an idea of what I mean.

Our daughter had been studying the Beethoven Fourth Piano Concerto and was scheduled to perform it as part of an important competition in Colorado. The history of that study was not always smooth. Earlier that year we had visited Lara at a summer music camp and attended a master class where she was to play the first movement of the concerto before a group of fellow students. In such a class the instructor—in this case a remarkably demanding teacher—usually critiques and comments as the student plays, stopping, coaching, and generally questioning and guiding the performance. This particular concerto opens with the piano alone and without the orchestra, in an extraordinary announcement of the theme, which is then followed by a response from the full orchestra. The teacher had announced to our daughter, "When you play that first chord, everyone will know what that performance will mean," and then she asked, "So what do you want to do with this piece? What is it about?" The Beethoven Fourth Piano Concerto is not exactly program music; it is not about a cloudburst or the ocean or a sunset. So the unexpected question was obviously unsettling to the poor girl at the piano who had, with this piece at least, been more concerned with notes than with ideas. But the teacher was unsympathetic and insistent, and kept pressing the question before allowing the performance to go on. Unable to satisfy her instructor, Lara, now almost in tears, could hardly play at all for the rest of the class, and at the end of her portion of the master class escaped to the back of the room in deep disappointment.

Many months of practice later, she was now in Colorado, preparing to play that same concerto in competition with some of the best young pianists from the Western United States. As one can easily imagine, such a competition is an extraordinarily intense environment: nervous performers are pacing back and forth, some with gloves on their precious hands, waiting their turn before the judges; others are with teachers giving passionate, whispered last-minute instructions; there are self-congratulatory, budding prima-donnas talking about the performance they are about to give; and, above all, are the scales, the runs, and the thunderous chords emanating from the warm-up rooms where the musicians work over shaky passages and loosen their fingers as they try to get the adrenaline under control. Everyone's attention is tied to the concert hall where, halfway back, the three judges, alone in the otherwise empty hall, await the next performer. The rooms, the halls, and above all the performance auditorium are electric with the intensity of the moment.

This is the environment in which Lara was to perform. A half an hour or so before her scheduled appearance, she asked for a priesthood blessing of peace. And then her mother and I left her alone in the warm-up room and made our way to the auditorium and the back row where a few family members and friends were allowed to quietly observe the proceedings.

At the scheduled time, her name was announced, Lara stepped onto the stage, and, with her sister at the accompanying piano, took her place at the keyboard of the concert grand. The judges said nothing, just nodded the go-ahead. But then, Lara didn't play. Instead of beginning the concerto, she just sat at the piano for what seemed to me like an eternity, even though it couldn't have been more than fifteen or twenty seconds. Finally—slowly and deliberately—she raised her hands to the keyboard, and that first chord rose from the piano as if by magic. Then the notes of the opening theme filled the hall, and as the accompanying piano followed with the orchestral response, I had the sense that something truly remarkable was happening. As the concerto continued, that feeling grew, and a sense of peace and joy that was almost palpable filled the auditorium. I could see the judges listening and writing their comments, but as the music went on, they wrote less and less and listened more and more to what was developing in the music. Eventually, they seemed to quit writing altogether; they put their pencils down, leaned back, and just listened with obvious pleasure. I knew they felt what we were feeling—the remarkable spirit of this piece.

After the glorious finale, Lara left the stage, and we hurried quickly to the foyer to meet her. She was smiling and obviously happy about what had just happened. We were deeply pleased as well. After the hugs and kisses and congratulations, I asked Lara about those suspenseful seconds of contemplation before she began to play. And then she told us of her remarkable experience as she waited for her turn to perform.

When we left her in the warm-up room before the performance, she was about to continue to rehearse some difficult sections of the concerto, but, knowing the benefit at this point would be minimal, she decided instead to read her scriptures. The Book of Mormon has very little to say about either Beethoven or playing the piano. So this was simply a continuation of a practice rooted in family experience and personal habit, a habit of daily scripture reading. She just opened the pages where the yellow ribbon marked her stopping point from the day before, Helaman, chapter 5. This is the account of two great missionaries, Lehi and Nephi, their imprisonment, their deliverance, and the miraculous bestowal of the Holy Ghost upon them and the people around them. As Lara read, she came to verse 44: "And Nephi and Lehi were in the midst of them; yea, they were encircled about; yea, they were as if in the midst of a flaming fire, yet it did harm them not, neither did it take hold upon the walls of the prison; and they were filled with *that joy which is unspeakable and full of glory*" (emphasis added). "That's it!" Lara said. "That is what this concerto is all about—'that joy which is unspeakable and full of glory!'" Those words from the Book of Mormon were the answer that she didn't have earlier that summer; they articulated for her the "meaning" of that concerto. And that was what she was thinking about in the seconds before she performed as she bowed her head and let those words from the Book of Mormon pass through her mind; and that was what we all felt as she played—a "joy which is unspeakable and full of glory!"

I learned something from that experience. The Lord does care about our "daily walk." He knows that we need help on Monday morning as much as we do on Sunday morning. And while our Sabbaths are profoundly significant, our Tuesdays, Wednesdays, and Thursdays are not exactly unimportant in His eyes. The Lord cares about what we do and what happens to us in the classroom, in the committee room, in the concert hall, on the freeway, and on the soccer field, in the daytime and in the nighttime, at home or away from home, at the computer or at the piano. His desire is to be with us always, and the scriptures— those sacred God-given texts—are an appointed means for His guiding and blessing us as we struggle and work through the wilderness and deserts and labors of our own mortal lives.

Those who let the standard works be their Liahonas, who establish the daily habit of soul-filling scripture study, have guidance in times of crisis or challenge, but additionally, they enjoy an extra facet to their lives. They develop a vocabulary of extraordinary expression, a language of the Spirit, the words of which can give form to testimony, to feelings of hope and love and faith that would otherwise struggle to be born or perhaps subside or wither and die in the ineptitude of one's own poor ability to say exactly how he feels. Those who know the scriptures have a powerful means of expression upon which the Spirit can draw.

For instance, I remember with extraordinary gladness the morning of one daughter's wedding when as her fiancé met her on their way to the temple he reached out, took her hand, and repeated spontaneously and with great spiritual exuberance, "Come ye, and let us go up to the mountain of the Lord, to the house of the God of Jacob; and he will teach us of his ways, and we will walk in his paths" (Isaiah 2:3). Those words captured the spirit of that wedding day and that young couple's mutual hope and future in a way that no other words could. But the words were not necessarily prepared *just for* that occasion. Those words were there *on* that occasion because of a young man's lifetime of living with and by the scriptures.

Furthermore, an intimacy with the scriptures provides a

repertoire of passages on which the Spirit can draw to enhance and magnify what are already sweet spiritual encounters. How often, for instance, have we come to the end of a particularly blest occasion and repeated Peter's extraordinary understatement, "it is good for us to be here" (Matthew 17:4), feeling as we did so that we might have at least a little something in common with that great Apostle. Indeed, to be one of a company of those who have regularly exerted themselves in studying the words and expressions and experiences of scripture makes possible life-changing experiences. Full-time missionaries live in just such a company, and their daily scripture study helps explain, at least in part, the wonderful work they accomplish. As a matter of course, we feel the need to turn to scripture as a capstone to many of our spiritual experiences, and if we are in a state of scriptural readiness with our reservoirs full, the Lord can indeed open the spiritual headgates of His living water and fill our hearts to the brim and overflowing.

One instance: recently, a few of our family were traveling in the Holy Land with some friends and neighbors, and found ourselves at the end of a typically full day an hour or so before sunset just inside the walls of the Old City of Jerusalem. Since our scheduled activities were finished, some were returning to the hotel while others sought out special museums or favorite sites that were not part of our scheduled activities. As we stood on the old street mulling over our possibilities, I asked our tour guide, Truman Madsen, about places where he liked to go to ponder the events and experiences we had talked about. He mentioned Gethsemane. It was nearby; we were scheduled to visit there on our last day, but Truman suggested that a preview beforehand would not be inappropriate. So with our tour guide leading the way, a small handful of us walked through the ancient city gate, dodged across the asphalt street, and made our way over to Gethsemane.

As we got there, instead of following the path to the right, the part where most of the tourists go, Truman led us left, and persuaded the kindly gentleman who was just locking the gate for the day to allow us into the less popular but more peaceful western section. We found a little bench and a box and sat together by one of the olive trees. The high solid walls shut out the traffic so we could hear the bird calls from the trees around us, and the lengthening shadows in the golden light of evening gave the whole place an atmosphere of tranquility, holiness, and peace. We visited together softly, speaking quietly of our new understandings and profound feelings regarding the event that had taken place near where we sat. We sang a hymn. Our hearts were full, and so were our eyes. Then as though responding to the unexpressed thoughts in all our hearts, our daughter Melinda opened the Book of Mormon and began to read words that were on the minds of several as we sat there together, words well known and familiar to everyone there in that little circle: "And behold, he shall be born of Mary, at Jerusalem. . . . And he shall go forth, suffering pains and afflictions and temptations of every kind; and this that the word might be fulfilled which saith he will take upon him the pains and the sicknesses of his people. And he will take upon him death, that he may loose the bands of death which bind his people; and he will take upon him their infirmities, that his bowels may be filled with mercy, according to the flesh, that he may know according to the flesh how to succor his people according to their infirmities" (Alma 7:10–12). Like no other expression, those words from Alma gave voice to our struggling feelings on that extraordinary evening. More literally than I could have ever expected, those sacred words from Alma had indeed "pointed for us a straight course" and confirmed and affirmed the delicious sweetness of the "eternal bliss" that we touched for a few moments that night. I will be forever grateful for that experience and the scriptural preparation that made it possible.

Sometimes as I lie awake at night trying to sort out the confusion and clutter of my post-modern life, I think of Lehi and his family and their concerns as they prepared to launch forth into the wilderness. I too am a pilgrim, and even though I don't carry the burden of the house of Joseph on my shoulders, I do carry the house of Neal Lambert, and that includes Anne and those eight daughters and their husbands and their children. We too have our wilderness to negotiate. It is not a place of sand and ravines and mountains, nor do we eat much raw meat. Nevertheless, we too at times wander and get lost—sometimes from our faith, sometimes from our faithful family. We too can feel cold, and hungry, and separated. We too long for the right words to guide those around us, and to tell them of our joy in our testimonies. That is why we too rejoice that the Lord in His goodness, has given us the means to bring us through the straight and narrow way and home to Him. As He gave Lehi and Nephi the Liahona so He has given us our own "directors." Our task is to move through our course by carefully considering the words that are written on them, and then following them "according to the directions" that are written, remembering "not to be slothful because of the easiness of the way," but always to "look that [we] might live" (Alma 37:46), for "thus we see that by small means the Lord can bring about great things" (1 Nephi 16:29).

CHAPTER 14

THE GOOD SAMARITAN AS A MODEL FOR FAMILY LIFE

H. Wallace Goddard

Jesus just keeps surprising us. In stories that seem shopworn and even trite, we discover truths that are powerful, pertinent, and unexpected. For example, there is hardly a more familiar story than that of the good Samaritan found in Luke 10. Let's consider the remarkable lessons for family life that can be learned from Jesus' familiar parable and His actions in teaching it.

"And, behold, a certain lawyer stood up and tempted him—" we're off to a good start. We are all tempted and tested in family life!— "saying, Master, what shall I do to inherit eternal life?" (v. 25).

Jesus did not react to the dishonesty of the question. Nor did He play to the weak side of the questioner. Notice how wisely Jesus crafted his response to the inquisitor: "What is written in the law? how readest thou?" (v. 26). Jesus invited the lawyer to cite the law.

H. Wallace Goddard is an associate professor of family and human development at Utah State University. He has studied teen problem behaviors and written The Great Self Mystery *to help teens discover and use their talents. He and his wife, Nancy, have three children and have had twenty foster children during their married life. He is also the author of* The Frightful and Joyous Journey of Family Life. *He has twice served as bishop.*

In family life we are often wise to follow this example. Sometimes a child will test us with an indignant declaration, such as, "Brent was shooting rubber bands in school today!" We may or may not suspect that the statement is autobiographical. While it does no good to second-guess the meaning of the question, it is often wise to invite the child's commentary. "Hmmm. You are a student at the school. What do you think about that?" As we give our children a chance to process their own feelings about the action, they may find their own answers.

After Jesus asked about the law, the lawyer replied to Jesus' query with familiar words: "Thou shalt love the Lord thy God with all thy heart, and with all thy soul, and with all thy strength, and with all thy mind; and thy neighbour as thyself" (v. 27).

Jesus acknowledged the answer: "Thou hast answered right: this do, and thou shalt live" (v. 28). But Jesus did not launch a follow-up lecture. He allowed the interest and maturity of the lawyer to drive the conversation, a wise course for us in families.

"But [the lawyer], willing to justify himself, said unto Jesus, And who is my neighbour?" (v. 29). Jesus clearly recognized the slippery intent of the lawyer (just as we often do with our children), but rather than confront and lecture him, He taught and invited him with a story that challenges us all.

"A certain man went down from Jerusalem to Jericho." Notice that, in this account, we have no identifying information about the central character of the story. Why are we given no detail about that poor man who made the lonely trek to Jericho? Because that traveler represents you and me and our partners and our children in our journeys of life. He is every man and every woman and every child.

The verse continues: "and fell among thieves, which stripped him of his raiment, and wounded him, and departed, leaving him half dead." What a perfect description of what every person experiences in the course of mortality! We all get injured and left alone along our treacherous journey of life. If we are sensitive parents, we notice that our children sometimes feel very alone and very hurt at regular intervals. If we are sensitive as partners, we look beyond our own pains and struggles to notice our partner's needs.

But, if we are operating at the telestial level, we will be as the thieves. We will strip family members of their self-respect, wound them with our accusations, and depart, leaving them half dead. It sounds so awful that we hardly imagine that we would treat each other that way. I wish I could say that I have not treated my dear wife and sweet children in such telestial ways.

When our daughter Emily was younger, maybe nine or ten years of age, and would ask to go to a friend's house to play, I would provide clear expectations about her returning time. Because I knew that Emily was usually late returning from any playdate, I advised her in the most ominous tones that she should be home at the designated time or she would face the consequences. I knew even as I expressed the demand that it would be hard for her to be home on time. I knew that she was a person who gets so involved in what she is doing that she loses track of time. "But she needs to learn to be responsible!" was my justification. One would think that my own chronic inability to get anywhere on time for the same reasons as Emily would make me more sympathetic to her. But the faults that we hate in ourselves we often hate even more in our children.

When Emily's appointed return time came I was standing watch at the door. As the minutes passed, making her later and later, I practiced my speech about consequences and responsibility and trust, and the longer I waited the more I added to the vitriol and the consequences. It was commonly fifteen or twenty minutes after the appointed time when Emily sauntered in with a smile on her face, quite unaware of her impending doom. I met her with hands on hips and began the lecture: "Emily! Did we not have an agreed time for your return? Did I not make it clear? When are you going to learn?" And I would threaten or impose some consequence, maybe grounding for a week. Now it embarrasses me to think about my self-righteous indignation.

All of this may seem fairly mild. I never hit Emily. And I never called her names. But I am now keenly aware that I left her stripped of self-respect and wounded. Can you imagine that I would injure and insult my little girl for doing the very thing that I regularly do? Any time we injure others for our own satisfaction or unholy indignation, we are operating as the ancient thieves—on a telestial level. We are injuring others with utter disregard. And we sometimes aggravate the sin by justifying our acts under the guise of noble purpose. Where will our children turn for comfort and healing?

Back to Luke 10:31. "And by chance there came down a certain priest that way." Ahhh! We are hopeful! Priests are those people in the community commissioned to see to the well-being of the people. Certainly he will care for the injured one.

"And when he saw him, he passed by on the other side." Yikes! Why would he do such a thing? He did not merely pass by, he went out of his way to avoid the disagreeable sight. What was he thinking? Maybe: "What a shame that people would be out on this dangerous road alone. Doesn't he know any better? What a fool! This is the natural consequence of such a foolish decision. I hope he learns a lesson. Besides, he is not in my ward." There is a cool detachment, maybe even some condescension in such a response.

Here comes the next passerby. Certainly he will stop. After all, he is a Levite, one who represents the people to the Lord in sacred ceremonies in the temple of God. "And likewise a Levite, when he was at the place, came and looked on him, and passed by on the other side." Was ceremonial cleanliness more important to the Levite than godly compassion? What a bitter irony! If the injured one was conscious, he must have been desperate. The holiest members of his community had passed him by. Would no one have pity on one as miserable and helpless as he?

The actions of the priest and Levite might be seen as terrestrial responses to suffering. Terrestrials are "honorable." They value fairness, reason, and consequences. Very often we humans feel wonderfully noble when we get to this level. It is, after all, much better than the telestial behavior that is the "natural" response of a person in this world.

I could have responded to Emily's lateness on this terrestrial level. Rather than attack her with accusation I might have calmly imposed consequences. "Emily, when you decide to break the law, you decide to take a consequence. I must respect your decision to be late by keeping you from Betsy's for two weeks." If I deliver this message in the spirit of fairness and without attack, then I may be operating on the terrestrial level. Most of the parenting programs of the world act as if this is as good as parenting ever gets: fairness, consequences, learning the lessons of life.

I remember the recommendation of an expert for dealing with children. If your pre-schooler is playing with toys when a neighbor child comes to invite your child to play, "you should stand at the door, clearly stating the rule, 'you can go out and play as soon as you put away all your toys.'"

That seems only fair. *Only* fair. But not helpful. What would your reaction be if your employer stood at the door at quitting time and said to you, "You may leave as soon as you clean up your space." Most of us would revolt against the embedded insult. We might clean up our space but we would thereafter resist our employer in subtle ways. Terrestrial behavior has the spirit of managing rather than inviting. It feels insulting rather than appreciating.

Like our response to a controlling boss, the confronted child may pout, throw a tantrum, or resist in subtle ways. Fairness, by itself, will never get us to the place we want to go with family relationships. So, if such confrontations are unproductive, how can we teach our children obedience and still treat them with respect? Every good grandmother knows the answer. So does the good Samaritan.

It would often appear that we have no hope as we weaken, like the wounded traveler, at the side of the road. "But a certain Samaritan, as he journeyed, came where he was" (v. 33). But certainly we will not get help from a Samaritan. They are half-breed pretenders to the great religious tradition. They are the lowest of the low. They are strangers and foreigners.

Yet, "when [the Samaritan] saw him, he had compassion on him." The first response of this distasteful stranger is compassion. He looks on our injuries with empathy. He might rightly claim that we brought the misery on ourselves. He might rightly claim that he has no responsibility for us. But he looks on us with the compassion characteristic of God. Joseph Smith taught: "But while one portion of the human race is judging and condemning the other without mercy, the Great Parent of the universe looks upon the whole of the human family with a fatherly care and paternal regard; He views them as His offspring, and without any of those contracted feelings that influence the children of men."[1]

While we would not expect this Samaritan passerby to do more than feel saddened by our plight, again we are surprised. The Samaritan "went to him, and bound up his wounds, pouring in oil and wine, and set him on his own beast, and brought him to an inn, and took care of him" (v. 34).

Wow! The stranger brings all of his resources to bear in healing us, the injured ones! He binds up our wounds. He is, after all One who is touched by every pain and infirmity that we ever suffer. The offensive Samaritan clearly represents Jesus.

Hugh Nibley teaches us that no ancient Jew could have misunderstood the ceremonial implications of "pouring in oil and wine." The alert reader recognizes sacred, even sacramental, emblems. Today, when we think of the oil, we recall hands laid on heads for healing. We think of anointing and dedicating our whole lives to sacred purposes. When we think of the wine, we remember His weekly invitation to "come boldly unto the throne of grace, that we may obtain mercy, and find grace to help in time of need" (Hebrews 4:16). We may come to Him boldly and hopefully because He has felt our infirmities. With His stripes we are healed. His compassion stretches to the infinities of time and space.

But there is still more. Jesus puts us on His beast and walks while we ride. What a model of meekness and humility! He, King of kings and Lord of lords, walks so that we may be carried to healing. And He who washes feet and wipes tears asks us to join Him in that same sacred, if thankless, task of blessing the weary and injured.

Jesus does not dump us at the first county hospital. He brings us to a safe place and tends to our healing. "And on the morrow when he departed, he took out two pence, and gave them to the host, and said unto him, Take care of him; and whatsoever thou spendest more, when I come again, I will repay thee" (v. 35).

When we are far enough healed that our recovery is assured, He leaves us in the care of loving servants to whom He has promised to repay every effort. And, having paid the infinite and eternal price, He is uniquely able to repay every kindness we provide to His injured and suffering ones. The uniquely appropriate if surprising gift He offers us for helping Him with healing His children is forgiveness of our sins. "For the sake of retaining a remission of your sins from day to day, that ye may walk guiltless before God—I would that ye should impart of your substance to the poor, every man according to that which he hath, such as feeding the hungry, clothing the naked, visiting the sick and administering to their relief, both spiritually and temporally, according to their wants" (Mosiah 4:26).

Notice that we are commanded to give "every man according to that which [we have]." Everything we have—our time, our talents, our resources—belongs to God for the blessing of His children.

What might be a celestial response to Emily's lateness problem? Since celestial parenting is motivated by love, it will first seek to understand the best way to be helpful and encouraging. If I had been prepared to be celestial in my dealings with Emily, I might have asked myself, "How can I set up Emily for success?" I think I might have suggested that she play until 5:00 P.M., and then I would come and get her. At the appointed time I could have walked over to Betsy's. On my way I might remind myself that it takes time for children to undertake transition from one activity to the next. So, when invited into Betsy's house, I might have asked Emily to show me what she had been doing. I might have listened with my heart in order to understand what is important and enjoyable to Emily. After Emily had several minutes to share her joy, I could invite her toward home, "I'm glad you have had so much fun with Betsy. Mom is at home getting dinner ready. Let's run home and help her." We could return home with joy, with Emily knowing that my love for her is stronger than the cords of death. That is what celestial parenting is about: blessing, redeeming, protecting, teaching, helping. And Heavenly Father is the perfect example of such parenting.

Of course the parenting behavior that works with ten-year-olds does not transfer directly for use with sixteen- and seventeen-year-olds. But the beauty of celestial parenting is that if we have been caring parents from the time of childhood, the teen years may be a dream as our children look to us as friends and guides. It is also possible that we will have especially difficult children (such as Laman and Lemuel) or that we will have struggled through years of imperfect parenting before we find better ways. But we are always wise to use compassion to understand our children who, as teens, may not want us to know that their acting-out is evidence of their painful injuries.

I used to assume that development was linear, that we progress from our natural-man telestiality toward fairness and terrestriality, then we add an appreciation of Jesus and move to the celestial level. I was wrong.

There is no ladder we can climb from terrestrial thinking and acting to celestial thinking and acting. We do not become celestial by adding a pinch of Jesus to a terrestrial life. At some point we simply throw ourselves on His merits, mercy, and grace. At some point we recognize that we may be able to keep ourselves from being the vilest of sinners, but if we are to be perfected, we must have His miraculous help (see D&C 76:69; Mosiah 3:19). The natural man must die and be born again as a spiritual being. That is the miracle. We do not climb out. He snatches us and delivers us to a new life.

"Who could have supposed that our God would have been so merciful as to have snatched us from our awful, sinful, and polluted state?" (Alma 26:17). We make ourselves humble (with a glad recognition of His great goodness and our own nothingness), and He makes us perfect: "[He] that exalteth himself shall be abased; and he that humbleth himself shall be exalted"! (Luke 18:14).

We may use determination and wisdom to bring ourselves from telestial reacting to terrestrial fairness. But we must have divine help to move to celestial goodness. It is not reasonable in this lone and dreary world to expect ourselves to operate on the celestial level all the time. But we can learn to avoid telestial behavior. With divine help we can spend more of our time on the celestial level.

Consider the application of this idea to the child who is invited by a neighbor child to go out and play. The celestial parent respects rules but celebrates people. So the celestial parent might say to the child, "Honey, won't that be fun to go out and play! That is so exciting. We need to put away the toys before you go out (and this is where parental discernment comes into play). I'll grab the toy box and help you get started." Or maybe the parent volunteers to get the child's shoes or jacket. The discerning parent knows what is the ideal action to help the child get started. It is, after all, our job to help children get what they want in a way that we feel good about. We should not see ourselves as heaven-authorized enforcers of the law, but as advocates, helpers, and teachers.

The celestial parent cares very much about law and obedience. But the message feels very different when delivered by someone who is an agent for love rather than control. We simply cannot win cooperation without deep respect for agency. The ideal context is redemption and healing rather than accusation and correction.

The same principle applies to marriage. It is so easy to be annoyed by things our partner does or fails to do. Based on years of experience with the person, we feel quite justified in judging our partner. Then we punish the person with shame and disdain. But that is not as it should be. Jesus invites us to have compassion for our partner. It is impossible for any one of us to fully understand the pain, struggle, and limitations that our partner feels. Jesus teaches us that only He, one of perfect knowledge and love, has the right to judge or punish (D&C 82:23), but we may bind up wounds with words of understanding: "It has been a hard day, hasn't it?" "It sounds as if you feel very alone." Sometimes the best healing is provided by ignoring our own pain and jumping in to help. We may know that our partner would feel very blessed if we volunteered to wash the dishes, care for the children, or join him or her in a walk. Often we know what we can do to heal and bless.

After blessing the lawyer with the remarkable story of the model Samaritan, Jesus invited him to identify the neighborly one. "Which now of these three, thinkest thou, was neighbour unto him that fell among the thieves? And he said, He that shewed mercy on him" (Luke 10:36–37).

He that showed mercy! How vital mercy is in family life. We forgive our parents of their flaws and limited knowledge. We forgive our partners for being human. We forgive our children for being children. Mercy is at the heart of family life.

Then said Jesus unto him, "Go, and do thou likewise" (v. 37). How do we apply His singular example to our family life?

1. *We approach every injured person with compassion rather than judgment.* It is so easy to want to fix family members. But, if we are to follow Jesus' example, we will bring our love and compassion to them rather than our agenda for adjustment. We are messengers for healing, encouraging, and redeeming.

2. *We share with them the principles of eternal life.* We teach them the true meaning of life: that we must know God. We teach them the great goodness of God. We teach them of our own nothingness. We teach them to call upon Father. And we teach them (primarily by our examples) to use every ounce of strength they possess to further Jesus' work of healing.

3. *We teach by being "wise as serpents, and harmless as doves"*

(Matthew 10:16). For most mortals it is a sizeable challenge to bring the purity and goodness that would qualify us to be described as "harmless as doves." In fact, we cannot do it without Father's help. But we must not neglect the other dimension: be "wise as serpents." Most of our preaching, moralizing, explaining, and cajoling makes our children crazy. If we have the recommended wisdom we will recognize when the approach is not working. Especially with young children, it is better to give simple and reasonable choices than lengthy and demeaning lectures.

4. *We draw on the miraculous power of His redemptiveness.* Each of us suffers injuries in mortality that go far beyond any mortal's ability to heal. But we are not left without hope. We have access to the power of a perfect healer. One of Satan's favorite lies is that we must get our lives straightened out before Father will come to us. After all, He cannot look upon sin with the least degree of allowance. But, if we study scriptural examples seriously, we discover that it is our job to make ourselves humble. When we are humble, He makes us clean. When we are clean, He comes to us and fills us up with the divine.

His perfect pattern is evident. Left to our own telestial inclinations, we are small, peevish, shrewish, judgmental, impatient, and self-serving. But, when we are filled with Him, we become new creatures. Not only do we feel more peace and joy, but we also are agents of His perfect love. President Ezra Taft Benson reminded us that "men and women who turn their lives over to God will discover that He can make a lot more out of their lives than they can. He will deepen their joys, expand their vision, quicken their minds, strengthen their muscles, lift their spirits, multiply their blessings, increase their opportunities, comfort their souls, raise up friends, and pour out peace. Whoever will lose his life in the service of God will find eternal life (see Matthew 10:39)."[2] The most important thing we can do to become good parents is to be filled with the Perfect Parent.

The parable of the Good Samaritan is only one of dozens of stories lived or taught by the Master. In every story are wise and inspiring messages that can help us be messengers of divine goodness in our families. May God bless us to find and use His great teachings as we strive to love as He loves.

NOTES

1. Joseph Smith, *The Teachings of Joseph Smith*, ed. Larry E. Dahl and Donald Q. Cannon (Salt Lake City: Bookcraft, 1997), p. 16.
2. Ezra Taft Benson, *The Teachings of Ezra Taft Benson* (Salt Lake City: Bookcraft, 1988), p. 361.

CHAPTER 15

THE PATTERN OF FAITH AND JOLTS OF JOY: SPIRITUAL SURPRISES

Richard H. Cracroft

I stood before them, at the end of a large *Bierstube* on an upper floor of the Munichholz Hotel in Steyr, Austria, enjoying once more the kind of spiritual surprise which has startled my life with refreshing frequency. "As all have not faith," I suppose the Lord has decided in my case, "let us give this man—and his kind—occasional jolts of joy. Otherwise, he'll never make it!"

So there I was, on a wintry Sunday morning in 1957, presenting a missionary discussion in my eight-month-old missionary German to a small group of Austrians in a cold and cluttered barroom carefully guarded by an Austrian plainclothes policeman ("plainclothes" meaning a slick leather trenchcoat, a slouch hat, and an unchanging expression).

Yet in the midst of this presentation on the need for a Savior in our lives, I was suddenly overwhelmed (not for the first time in those eight months) by the beauty of the plan I was outlining, by the wondrous nature of the Savior's role therein, and by the

---

Richard H. Cracroft is a professor of English at BYU and director of the Center for the Study of Christian Values in Literature. Currently a bishop, he has served as a stake president and president of the Switzerland Zürich Mission. Richard and his wife, Janice, live in Provo. They are the parents of three children: Richard, Jeffrey, and Jennifer.

monumental significance of His role and that plan for me, my
companion, and everyone in that room (including the cop), that
city, Austria, and the entire world. Suddenly I transcended into
the "O that I were an angel" or the "O Jerusalem" experience
and *felt* anew the thrill of what I had come to know as the Holy
Spirit's workings on me—the welcome (but somehow different)
chill up the spine; the fine, cold (but somehow different) sweat
on my forehead; and the slight tremor of joy throughout my
body. All of these signs affirmed to me that I was, at the
moment, a testator of eternal truth, a witness for Jesus Christ. I
thrilled.

Yet even as I looked at my minuscule "congregation" and
saw the confirming Spirit working on each face (I'm, not sure
about the cop)—even then I was blessed with another affirming
kind of testimony: suddenly I (or some part of me) was out of
my body, at the back of the room, elevated in the corner, watching the whole event at a remove. I was looking at the backs of
my friends; I was seeing *me* standing before that attentive group,
while the other *me* in the rear corner was filled with a wondrous
confirmation that what the young man was saying, in fervent but
labored German, was true.

That other, somehow spiritually objective *me* was filled with
amazement at the changes which those truths had wrought upon
that young man who, a year earlier, was struggling with himself,
drifting, frustrated and purposeless, in and out of the gospel net.
At that moment I realized Joy. And like Enos, I knew it was but
a type of the joy which comes to every man and woman who,
through the ministrations of the Holy Ghost, *realizes* Jesus
Christ, and God, and the vision of the life of the Spirit.

Then, suddenly I was back in my earth-bound body, looking
again through my own corporeal-spiritual eyes into the faces and
hearts of the little congregation. And I knew, more than ever,
that all of those truths which we encompass by the words, "The
Gospel," were *really* true—true in a sense far beyond what I had
hitherto comprehended; true in the sense of becoming, as my
mission president, the late Jesse R. Curtis always said, "truer by

the minute"; true in the sense that such truths are accessible by seeking unchanging patterns of faith which lead to knowledge and surprises of the Spirit—thrilling road signs on the course to eternal life.

So it has gone, since then, with me and the gospel and faith and life. Always endowed with a love for good books and for writing, I early opted for an English major (and was the only football player at Salt Lake City's East High School who joined the Pegasus [Literary] Club), a career as a teacher, and a lifetime of learning. This course was right, I felt, and I knew it was fun. Much later, I learned that such a course is termed "intellectual," a label with which I have never felt comfortable, implying as it seemed to that I was much brighter than I knew myself to be, and also implying an independence from God that I would ever shun.

Then I ran head-on into college—and into the company of brilliant young men (and a handful of teachers) who burningly disbelieved and who urged intellectual independence, themselves disdaining any spiritual dependence on God or His Church. They led me to drink from the heady draughts of doubt. Amidst my own short-lived rebellion against Church and familial standards (which, it soon became apparent by my own guilt, had become *my* incontrovertible standards), I pondered life. My late-night thoughts were highly unoriginal self-catechisms regarding my own beliefs: Is there a purpose in the universe? Is this purpose embodied in a God? Does this God or purpose care about man? When we die, will we live again? If so, how? where? If we live again is there a judgment on our social conduct during mortality? Is Jesus Christ truly what He is purported to be? Is prayer in His name listened to by anyone? Would God or Christ really answer the prayers of individuals? Are prophets individuals who have received answers? Was Joseph Smith such a receptor? Is David O. McKay? (How I loved him!) I would then ponder the topics on which my friends could argue for hours: evolution, the historicity of Jesus of Nazareth,

the personal weaknesses of Joseph Smith and other Church leaders, polygamy, the Mountain Meadows massacre, the Blacks (in
those days it was "the Negroes") and the priesthood, the divinity
of the Book of Mormon—and I was troubled by all of these topics. And so was everyone else I knew.

Night after night I would lie abed rehearsing this catechism,
reviewing the arguments of my respected and articulate friends,
their antitheses pounding in my ears. But, somehow, I kept on
praying: each time, something within led me to conclude my
vigil by kneeling in prayer. I would set aside my violations of my
own standards, set aside my intellectual upheavals, and would
pray to God just as I had been trained—for comfort, hope, and
direction.

Amidst my follies, I also continued to attend Church meetings, where a wise bishop overlooked my hypocrisy (or more
simply and kindlier—*confusion*) and allowed me to become a
senior ward teacher and a Sunday School teacher. I continued to
perform both functions scrupulously, thereby keeping a finger-
nail grip on the outward Church, even as I was probing my
inward beliefs. That same wise bishop urged but did not nag, set
some tolerable and tolerant goals, and finally led me to see a
course on which I would have to make some tentative decisions
about my nightly catechism.

I decided that none of my questions could be decided by the
intellect. I would have to opt for faith; and I soon realized that
opting for faith was impossible without commitment. So I opted
to test faith by living all of the commandments. I was amazed
how soon I felt so very well about everything, and it was only a
matter of days before I knew that I must also opt for the missionary experience.

I dreaded this experience, stretching out before me like a
thirty-month sentence to Siberia. But I was also intrigued. I felt
that a mission was, in fact, put up or shut up time for me, but
also for the Lord. Frankly, I did not expect very much out of the
missionary experience; but if faith precedes the miracle, I rea-
soned, I'd better see a miracle or two before long.

They came! I went to Austria and Switzerland, determined to place hard work on the altar. To my surprise, hard work led to increased faith; then, increasingly, to surprises of the Spirit, to promised miracles, as the Lord met the conditions of our bargain, "irrevocably decreed" as it had apparently been, "before the foundations of the world"—a bargain based in the pattern of faith, so simple, so true, and so available to everyone. My mission became a marvelous unfolding of my spirit, a time of discovering the patterns of joy.

I delighted to find that my companions and I could actually teach others the pattern. I soon saw the pattern I had just worked through repeated, with some variation, in the life of one of those we brought into the Church from that little group in Steyr, Austria (incidentally, most of the group in the *Bierstube* joined the Church within the following weeks).

Brother Karl, a leader in the Seventh-Day Adventist congregations in Upper Austria, first came to our attention when his wife, interested in our series of Tuesday lectures, invited us to meet him. Alert to the challenge, we armed ourselves with Sabbath-day scriptural references. Then, humble, fearful, and fasting, we rode our bikes to our meeting at his home. As we feared, our lesson on the Godhead was immediately challenged, and we allowed ourselves to be turned from our purpose to discussing the Sabbath. In the middle of the futile battle, however, a powerful inspiration struck my companion (whom I love today as I did then). He sent me, Doubting Dick, to my bicycle saddlebags to fetch the plan of salvation outline which I had carefully sketched on a roll of oilcloth. Since this was "my lesson," I began, now more fearful than ever, to teach those familiar concepts which we generally reserved until the second month of our visits. I wondered about my companion's inspiration.

But not for long. As I moved through the lesson, Brother Karl began to supply the supporting scriptures—even some we hadn't thought of. As I attempted to explain the various aspects of the plan, he would gently interrupt and clarify the concepts to his wife and older children. And when I broached the need for vicarious baptism for the dead, he jumped to his feet, tears springing to his eyes, and loudly recited 1 Corinthians 15:29 ("Else what shall they do which are baptized for the dead"). "I have studied for years," he cried "to find out what this scripture meant, and now two young Americans make it crystal clear." Surprise: chill up the spine, cold sweat on the forehead, a body tremor. For all of us. Brother Karl was converted that evening and, with his wife, was baptized a month later.

I love him yet for the insights he taught me. One of us asked him in a later meeting how he had been able to overlook his strong feelings about the Sabbath. "I was faced by a larger, more comprehensive truth in which I had utmost faith," he said, "and I couldn't be bothered by lesser particulars." He knew that if he followed the grander truth, the other, lesser truths would all, somehow, fall into place. He had learned the pattern.

This spiritual surprise and the ensuing miracles also occurred in the life of Margarete, a sweet sixteen-year-old girl who also sat in that *Bierstube* on that long-ago morning. After a wonderful and profound conversion she joined the Church, and, through a series of inspired actions, was assisted in fleeing a terrible home environment to live among Church members in Switzerland. Just a few days later, she met a handsome young visitor from Germany who had joined the Church six months earlier and had chanced to come to Bass, Switzerland, for his vacation. They were married in the Swiss Temple two years later, have watched each of their children marry in the temple, and continue to live happily in Germany, where he has served as bishop. The couple visited us recently, still rejoicing in their conversion and in each other, a joy which has also been renewed through a host of surprises of the Spirit. They know the pattern.

I believe, at least in part, because I have watched the old patterns work in my life and in the lives of others. I believe because the patterns are testworthy. The individual makes a gesture toward belief and faith; the Spirit bears witness; the miracle follows; then the surprises of the Spirit crop up from time to time to remind the believer that though he or she is twenty or forty or sixty years out from home, our Father will send a spark, a surprise, or a shock of recognition as if to say, "Here, my child, here is a whiff of truth, a thrill of remembrance, a tangible something to remind you—for a moment—that I'm here; that you're on course; that your feet are still treading, however imperfectly, the paths which will lead to joy in mortality and in eternity."

At least it has been so for me. I became an academic, a professor, a dean; I have learned the (in)appropriate skepticism; I have actively pursued *truth* (lowercase), and frankly enjoyed the pursuit. But as an observer of others—not only as an academic but as a bishop, stake president, and mission president—I have learned to my own satisfaction that the truths found in the historical record are secondary to the larger, comprehensive gospel *Truths* (uppercase) found through faith—until those lesser truths find their larger spiritual context. It is a matter of perspective, and I find more joy and satisfaction in the larger, vertical perspective than in the narrower, horizontal view.

For me the pattern has always followed the course it took one afternoon in 1967, in the stacks of the library at the University of Wisconsin I was pursuing a book through the aisles of bookshelves when, to my surprise, I found myself in the Mormon section, which I had not discovered in two years of intensive library work. I looked at a number of newer books, books which I had not read. Suddenly, a spiritual craving overwhelmed me and I sat down at a carrel, realizing that though I was "active" and "faithful," I had not made any real effort to study the gospel for over two years. I read hungrily all afternoon in the books I had found, then went home for a chat with my wife, confessing to her that I had allowed an embarrassing imbalance to develop in my life and had gradually shifted perspectives. I resolved to her that I would opt more strongly for the spiritual route, though I expressed concern that time and energy would be difficult to find, engaged as I was in completing my doctoral studies. Then another surprise (I shouldn't have been surprised by then—I knew the pattern): that Sunday, the bishop called me to be the new seminary teacher; I accepted, even before I learned there was a small but welcome stipend. Suddenly I found myself, each weekday evening, spending from 10:30 P.M. until midnight studying the New Testament. It was a gift from the Lord, in answer to an enlivened faith, a gift which enabled me to regain my spiritual equipoise.

I have found, then, that even a slight gesture toward faith will beget opportunities to put one's life in harmony with God's pattern—regardless of mortal pressures. Indeed, every time I have opted to place faith above other matters, I have been almost instantly rewarded with spiritual surprises, with growth, with joy. I believe in the pattern: opting for faith soon begets change and growth and opportunity. It works; how can I not believe? How much more important is this joy than the spiritual bruisings which I inevitably receive through criticism of leadership, policies, programs—and fellow mortals. I find I must soon hasten back to the pattern to find spiritual growth and refreshment.

That spiritual manifestation which I experienced in Austria is a rich memory for me yet, but it has been a memory reinforced through many such surprises which have repeatedly affirmed to me that opting for faith back in 1956 was the right course to belief and testimony and increased faith. It is not a new option, of course. Rather, it is the timeless and proven way of the spiritual race, from Adam through Abraham and Moses, Isaiah and Jeremiah, from Jesus to Peter and John and Paul; it is the way of spiritual men from Joseph Smith to Brigham Young to David O. McKay, and Gordon B. Hinckley; it is the way for every one of us mortals who desires to have his or her name inscribed in the Lamb's Book of Life.

I am a common man, a scene-sweller at best. Yet even in my relatively insignificant ministry, tucked away in Provo, Utah, and Zürich Switzerland, the Lord's will has been manifest and, with countless others who labor quietly in their ministries, I could present a rich catalogue of striking and wondrous surprises of the Spirit. Some time ago I was stopped on my way by a man who said, "That was quite a blessing you gave." He reminded me that four years before he had been given up for dead, with inoperable brain cancer; that I, who was then his stake president, had given him a blessing; that he had been cured—and had just then gotten around to telling me about it!

Again, he reminded me of the faith-pattern. I do not profess to have the gift of healing, but as I assess the list of persons whom I have blessed over several decades, I repeatedly find the old pattern of joyous surprise in which the Lord has reversed, abated, or slowed apparently mortal illnesses. I think of words which have crowded into my mouth at the bedside of several Saints certain to die, words which cry out against rational knowledge imparted by the doctor, words proclaiming healing or the promise of several more years of vigorous, productive life—and I wonder, but I no longer tremble, for the words are fulfilled.

I don't profess to know why He doesn't always heal, or why He often chooses to allow this young father or that mother or child to die while that one is spared, when to spare them all would seem merciful and just. I know only that we must "confess his hand in all things," understand our quaint perspective, and affirm that "blessed are the dead that die in the Lord" (D&C 63:49).

And I ponder the other surprises of the Spirit: the clear-cut instances of revelation I saw as stake president in selecting men to become bishops, manifestations so powerful that I could say "thus saith the Lord" in issuing those calls; or in selecting women to fill important callings in Relief Society, Primary, and the YWMIA—instances in which I could not take my mind or my pencil from a name on a list, a name I barely knew, until I resolved to issue the call; or instances in which it came clearly to me that the right name was not on the list. In one such case, I returned to fasting and prayer—with a deadline, only to hear my wife mention, five minutes before the deadline, the right person's name in an entirely different context, and receive the familiar chill up the spine and the confirmation I had sought. (Only to be told later that evening by the senior high councilor, while clearing the name, "Oh, I saw her in the store the other day and the Spirit said, 'There's the new president.'" "Why didn't you tell me?" I groused. "Why, the Lord's directing this stake; I knew you'd get the message soon enough.") So it went, time after time.

And I think of the intervention from beyond the grave: of the time when the recently deceased mother of a young missionary made her presence so powerfully known during the setting-apart that I finally had to acknowledge it in the blessing—and how the inactive father took me aside, pale and trembling, and said he had looked up and saw his deceased wife standing beside him. It made a difference in his life! And I think of the blessing of a believing but shattered alcoholic. Following the initial portion of the sealing blessing, his mother, also recently dead, literally took over the blessing. I was led to introduce her presence, to counsel the man to listen to the words of his mother—who spoke to him, through me, with all of the tender yet warning words she could pour from behind the veil. It was a humbling experience which my counselor and I will never forget.

These events are faithful realities. While they do not necessarily lead to belief, they affirm the pattern of faith, and they make vivid the actuality of the spiritual world. Collectively they overwhelm me and make it easy to believe such scriptural statements as "I beheld the heavens open. . . . And I saw the Lord, and he stood before my face, and he talked with me, even as a man talketh one with another, face to face" (Moses 7:3–4); or to believe the experience in that wooded grove, that modern Mount of Transfiguration, in which Joseph Smith, Jr., says, "I saw a pillar of light exactly over my head, above the brightness of the sun, [and] I saw two Personages, whose brightness and glory defy all description, standing above me in the air. One of them spake unto me, calling me by name and said, pointing to the other—This is My Beloved Son, Hear Him!" (JS–H 1:16–17)

Truth and testimony have flooded the earth—but not many desire to wet their feet. "Give me evidence," they cry, overlooking the testimonies of thousands now dead who have left a record of their witness, or the witnesses of hundreds among us whose testimonies appear in print, who bear witness in meetings, who offer us accounts of their spiritual surprises. I believe these testimonies are true and faithful, for they spring from the great pattern, from faith, and, when they are listened to by the faithful, live afresh, for the Spirit transforms their words into Living Water. And the word flows forth—and always shall—the word which answers the questions of my youthful catechism (and everyone's): There is a God—I have learned it. Jesus of Nazareth is His Only Begotten in the flesh—I know it. The prophets of God speak and have spoken truth—the Spirit whispers it. Joseph Smith is a prophet of God—God declares it. The Book of Mormon is a true witness of Christ—Christ affirms it. The Church of Jesus Christ of Latter-day Saints continues as the "only true and living Church" with which our Lord is well pleased—He has spoken it.

It is for us, then, to rejoice, give thanks, and endure in faith and in gratitude for the pattern, for those flashes of Truth which God in His grace grants His Saints. This witness, which has come through faith, is available to such as can be still, listen, and know that God is God and has all things in His sure hands, in which we must place ourselves, occasionally stirred by jolts of joy and faithfully awaiting the resolution.

INDEX